Nathaniel Hawthorne

Transformation

The Romance of Monte Beni

Nathaniel Hawthorne

Transformation
The Romance of Monte Beni

ISBN/EAN: 9783742814159

Manufactured in Europe, USA, Canada, Australia, Japa

Cover: Foto ©Andreas Hilbeck / pixelio.de

Manufactured and distributed by brebook publishing software (www.brebook.com)

Nathaniel Hawthorne

Transformation

TRANSFORMATION:

OR, THE

ROMANCE OF MONTE BENI.

BY

NATHANIEL HAWTHORNE,
AUTHOR OF "THE SCARLET LETTER," ETC. ETC.

IN THREE VOLUMES.

VOL. II.

LONDON:
SMITH, ELDER & CO., 65, CORNHILL.
M.DCCC.LX.

CONTENTS

OF THE SECOND VOLUME.

Chap.		Page
I. Miriam's Trouble		1
II. On the Edge of a Precipice		16
III. The Faun's Transformation		27
IV. The Burial Chaunt		46
V. The Dead Capuchin		64
VI. The Medici Gardens		80
VII. Miriam and Hilda		91
VIII. The Tower among the Apennines		112
IX. Sunshine		126
X. The Pedigree of Monte Beni		145
XI. Myths		167
XII. The Owl Tower		186
XIII. On the Battlements		201
XIV. Donatello's Bust		221
XV. The Marble Saloon		234
XVI. Scenes by the Way		255
XVII. Pictured Windows		278

THE ROMANCE OF MONTE BENI.

CHAPTER I.

MIRIAM'S TROUBLE.

As usual of a moonlight evening, several carriages stood at the entrance of this famous ruin, and the precincts and interior were anything but a solitude. The French sentinel, on duty beneath the principal archway, eyed our party curiously, but offered no obstacle to their admission. Within, the moonlight filled and flooded the great empty space; it glowed upon tier above tier of ruined, grass-grown arches, and made them even too distinctly visible. The splendour of the revelation took away that inestimable effect of dimness and mystery by which the imagination might be assisted to build a grander structure than the Coliseum, and to shatter it with a more picturesque decay. Byron's celebrated description is better than the reality. He beheld the scene in his mind's eye, through the witchery of many intervening years, and faintly illuminated it as if with starlight, instead of this broad glow of moonshine.

The party of our friends sat down, three or four of them on a prostrate column, another on a shapeless lump of marble, once a Roman altar; others on the steps of one of the Christian shrines. Goths and barbarians though they were, they chatted as gaily together as if they belonged to the gentle and pleasant race of people who now inhabit Italy. There was much pastime and gaiety just then in the area of the Coliseum, where so many gladiators and wild beasts had fought and died, and where so much blood of Christian martyrs had been lapt up by that fiercest of wild beasts, the Roman populace of yore. Some youths and maidens were running merry races across the open space, and playing at hide-and-seek a little way within the duskiness of the ground-tier of arches, whence, now and then, you could hear the half-shriek, half-laugh, of a frolicksome girl, whom the shadow had betrayed into a young man's arms. Elder groups were seated on the fragments of pillars and blocks of marble, that lay round the verge of the arena, talking in the quick, short ripple of the Italian tongue. On the steps of the great black cross in the centre of the Coliseum, sat a party, singing scraps of songs, with much laughter and merriment between the stanzas.

It was a strange place for song and mirth. That black cross marks one of the special blood-spots of the earth, where thousands of times over the dying gladiator fell, and more of human agony has been endured, for the mere pastime of the multitude than on the breadth of many battle-fields. From all this crime and suffering, however, the spot has derived a more than common sanctity. An inscription promises seven years' indulgence, seven years of remission from the pains of purgatory, and earlier enjoyment of heavenly bliss, for each separate kiss imprinted on the black cross. What better use could be made of life, after middle-age, when the accumulated sins are many, and the remaining temptations few, than to spend it all in kissing the black cross of the Coliseum!

Besides its central consecration, the whole area has been made sacred by a range of shrines, which are erected round the circle, each commemorating some scene or circumstance of the Saviour's passion and suffering. In accordance with an ordinary custom, a pilgrim was making his progress from shrine to shrine, upon his knees, and saying a penitential prayer at each. Light-footed girls ran across the path along which he crept, or sported with their friends close by the shrines where he was kneeling. The pilgrim took no heed, and the girls meant no irreverence;

for in Italy religion jostles along side by side with business and sport, after a fashion of its own; and people are accustomed to kneel down and pray, or see others praying between two fits of merriment, or between two sins.

To make an end of our description, a red twinkle of light was visible amid the breadth of shadow that fell across the upper part of the Coliseum. Now it glimmered through a line of arches, or threw a broader gleam, as it rose out of some profound abyss of ruin; now it was muffled by a heap of shrubbery which had adventurously clambered to that dizzy height; and so the red light kept ascending to loftier and loftier ranges of the structure, until it stood like a star where the blue sky rested against the Coliseum's topmost wall. It indicated a party of English or Americans paying the inevitable visit by moonlight, and exulting themselves with raptures that were Byron's, not their own.

Our company of artists sat on the fallen column, the pagan altar, and the steps of the Christian shrine, enjoying the moonlight and shadow, the present gaiety and the gloomy reminiscences of the scene, in almost equal share. Artists, indeed, are lifted by the ideality of their pursuits a little way off the earth, and are therefore able to catch the evanescent fragrance that floats in the atmosphere of life above the heads of the ordinary crowd. Even if they seem endowed with little imagination individually, yet there is a property, a gift, a talisman, common to their class, entitling them to partake somewhat more bountifully than other people in the thin delights of moonshine and romance.

"How delightful this is!" said Hilda; and she sighed for very pleasure.

"Yes," said Kenyon, who sat on the column, at her side. "The Coliseum is far more delightful, as we enjoy it now, than when eighty thousand persons sat squeezed together, row above row, to see their fellow-creatures torn by lions and tigers limb from limb. What a strange thought, that the Coliseum was really built for us, and has not come to its best uses till almost two thousand years after it was finished!"

"The Emperor Vespasian scarcely had us in his mind," said Hilda, smiling; "but I thank him none the less for building it."

"He gets small thanks, I fear, from the people whose bloody instincts he pampered," rejoined Kenyon. "Fancy a nightly assemblage of eighty thousand melancholy and remorseful ghosts, looking down from those tiers of broken arches, striving to repent of the savage pleasures which they once enjoyed, but still longing to enjoy them over again."

"You bring a Gothic horror into this peaceful moonlight scene," said Hilda.

"Nay, I have good authority for peopling the Coliseum with phantoms," replied the sculptor. "Do you remember that veritable scene in Benvenuto Cellini's autobiography, in which a necromancer of his acquaintance draws a magic circle—just where the black cross stands now, I suppose—and raises myriads of demons? Benvenuto saw them with his own eyes—giants, pigmies, and other creatures of frightful aspect, —capering and dancing on yonder walls. These spectres must have been Romans, in their lifetime, and frequenters of this bloody amphitheatre."

"I see a spectre now!" said Hilda, with a little thrill of uneasiness. "Have you watched that pilgrim, who is going round the whole circle of shrines, on his knees, and praying with such fervency at every one? Now that he has revolved so far in his orbit, and has the moonshine on his face, as he turns towards us, methinks I recognize him!"

"And so do I," said Kenyon. "Poor Miriam! Do you think she sees him?"

They looked round, and perceived that Miriam had risen from the steps of the shrine and disappeared. She had shrunk back, in fact, into the deep obscurity of an arch that opened just behind them.

Donatello, whose faithful watch was no more to be eluded than that of a hound, had stolen after her, and became the innocent witness of a spectacle that had its own kind of horror. Unaware of his presence, and fancying herself wholly unseen, the beautiful Miriam began to gesticulate extravagantly, gnashing her teeth, flinging her arms wildly abroad, stamping with her foot. It was as if she had stepped aside for an instant, solely to snatch the relief of a brief fit of madness. Persons in acute trouble, or labouring under strong excitement, with a necessity for concealing it, are prone to relieve their nerves in this wild way; although, when practicable, they find a more effectual solace in shrieking aloud.

Thus, as soon as she threw off her self-control, under the dusky arches of the Coliseum, we may consider Miriam as a mad woman, concentrating the elements of a long insanity into that instant.

"Signorina! signorina! have pity on me!" cried Donatello, approaching her—"this is too terrible!"

"How dare you look at me?" exclaimed Miriam, with a start; then, whispering below her breath, "men have been struck dead for a less offence!"

"If you desire it, or need it," said Donatello humbly, "I shall not be loth to die."

"Donatello," said Miriam, coming close to the young man, and speaking low, but still the almost insanity of the moment vibrating in her voice, "if you love yourself, if you desire those earthly blessings such as you, of all men, were made for, if you would come to a good old age among your olive-orchards and your Tuscan vines, as your forefathers did; if you would leave children to enjoy the same peaceful, happy, innocent life, then flee from me. Look not behind you! Get you gone without another word." He gazed sadly at her, but did not stir. "I tell you," Miriam went on, "there is a great evil hanging over me! I know it; I see it in the sky; I feel it in the air! It will overwhelm me as utterly as if this arch should crumble down upon our heads! It will crush you, too, if you stand at my side! Depart, then; and make the sign of the cross, as your faith bids you, when an evil spirit is nigh. Cast me off, or you are lost for ever."

A higher sentiment brightened upon Donatello's face, than had hitherto seemed to belong to its simple expression and sensuous beauty.

"I will never quit you," he said; "you cannot drive me from you."

"Poor Donatello!" said Miriam, in a changed tone, and rather to herself than him. "Is there no other that seeks me out—follows me—is obstinate to share my affliction and my doom—but only you! They call me beautiful; and I used to fancy that, at my need, I could bring the whole world to my feet. And, lo! here is my utmost need; and my beauty and my gifts have brought me only this poor, simple boy. Half-witted, they call him; and surely fit for nothing but to be happy. And I accept his aid! To-morrow, to-morrow, I will tell him all! Ah! what a sin to stain his joyous nature with the blackness of a woe like mine!"

She held out her hand to him, and smiled sadly as Donatello pressed it to his lips. They were now about to emerge from the depth of the arch; but, just then, the kneeling pilgrim, in his revolution round the orbit of the shrines, had reached the one on the steps of which Miriam had been sitting. There, as at the other shrines, he prayed, or seemed to pray. It struck Kenyon, however, who sat close by, and saw his face distinctly—that the suppliant was merely performing an enjoined penance, and without the penitence that ought to have given it effectual life. Even as he knelt, his eyes wandered, and Miriam soon felt that he had detected her, half hidden as she was within the obscurity of the arch.

"He is evidently a good Catholic, however," whispered one of the party. "After all, I fear we cannot identify him with the ancient pagan who haunts the catacombs."

MIRIAM'S TROUBLE. 13

"The doctors of the Propaganda may have converted him," said another; "they have had fifteen hundred years to perform the task."

The company now deemed it time to continue their ramble. Emerging from a side entrance of the Coliseum, they had on their left the Arch of Constantine, and, above it, the shapeless ruins of the Palace of the Cæsars; portions of which have taken shape anew, in mediæval convents and modern villas. They turned their faces cityward, and, treading over the broad flagstones of the old Roman pavement, passed through the Arch of Titus. The moon shone brightly enough within it, to show the seven-branched Jewish candlestick, cut in the marble of the interior. The original of that awful trophy lies buried, at this moment, in the yellow mud of the Tiber; and, could its gold of Ophir again be brought to light, it would be the most precious relic of past ages, in the estimation of both Jew and Gentile.

Standing amid so much ancient dust, it is

difficult to spare the reader the commonplaces of enthusiasm, on which hundreds of tourists have already insisted. Over this half-worn pavement, and beneath this Arch of Titus, the Roman armies had trodden in their outward march, to fight battles, a world's width away. Returning victorious, with royal captives and inestimable spoil, a Roman triumph, that most gorgeous pageant of earthly pride, had streamed and flaunted in hundred-fold succession over these same flag-stones, and through this yet stalwart archway. It is politic, however, to make few allusions to such a past; nor, if we would create an interest in the characters of our story, is it wise to suggest how Cicero's foot may have stepped on yonder stone, or how Horace was wont to stroll near by, making his footsteps chime with the measure of the ode that was ringing in his mind. The very ghosts of that massive and stately epoch have so much density, that the actual people of to-day seem the thinner of the two, and stand more ghost-like by the arches and columns, letting the rich sculpture be discerned through their ill-compacted substance.

The party kept onward, often meeting pairs and groups of midnight strollers like themselves. On such a moonlight night as this, Rome keeps itself awake and stirring, and is full of song and pastime, the noise of which mingles with your dreams, if you have gone betimes to bed. But it is better to be abroad, and take our own share of the enjoyable time; for the languor that weighs so heavily in the Roman atmosphere by day, is lightened beneath the moon and stars.

They had now reached the precincts of the Forum.

CHAPTER II.

ON THE EDGE OF A PRECIPICE.

"LET us settle it," said Kenyon, stamping his foot firmly down, "that this is precisely the spot where the chasm opened, into which Curtius precipitated his good steed and himself. Imagine the great, dusky gap, impenetrably deep, and with half-shaped monsters and hideous faces looming upward out of it, to the vast affright of the good citizens who peeped over the brim! There, now, is a subject, hitherto unthought of, for a grim and ghastly story, and, methinks, with a moral as deep as the gulf itself. Within it, beyond a question, there were prophetic visions—intimations of all the future calamities of Rome—shades of Goths and Gauls, and even of the French soldiers of to-day. It was a pity to close it up so soon! I would give much for a peep into such a chasm."

"I fancy," remarked Miriam, "that every person takes a peep into it in moments of gloom and despondency; that is to say, in his moments of deepest insight."

"Where is it, then?" asked Hilda. "I never peeped into it."

"Wait, and it will open for you," replied her friend. "The chasm was merely one of the orifices of that pit of blackness that lies beneath us, everywhere. The firmest substance of human happiness is but a thin crust spread over it, with just reality enough to bear up the illusive stage-scenery amid which we tread. It needs no earthquake to open the chasm. A footstep, a little heavier than ordinary, will serve; and we must step very daintily, not to break through the crust at any moment. By-and-by, we inevitably sink! It was a foolish piece of heroism in Curtius to precipitate himself there, in advance; for all Rome, you see, has been swallowed up in that gulf, in spite of him. The Palace of the Cæsars has gone down thither, with a hollow, rumbling sound of its fragments! All the temples have tumbled into it; and thousands of statues have been thrown after! All the armies and the triumphs have marched into the great chasm, with their martial music playing, as they stept over the brink. All the heroes, the statesmen, and the poets! All piled upon poor Curtius, who thought to have saved them all! I am loth to smile at the self-conceit of that gallant horseman, but cannot well avoid it."

"It grieves me to hear you speak thus, Miriam," said Hilda, whose natural and cheerful piety was shocked by her friend's gloomy view of human destinies. "It seems to me that there is no chasm, nor any hideous emptiness under our feet, except what the evil within us digs. If there be such a chasm, let us bridge it over with good thoughts and deeds, and we shall tread safely to the other side. It was the guilt of Rome, no doubt, that caused this gulf to open; and Curtius filled it up with his heroic self-sacrifice, and patriotism, which was the best virtue that the old Romans knew. Every wrong thing makes the gulf deeper; every right one helps to fill it up. As the evil of Rome was far more than its good, the whole commonwealth finally sank into it, indeed, but of no original necessity."

"Well, Hilda, it came to the same thing at last," answered Miriam, despondingly.

"Doubtless, too," resumed the sculptor (for his imagination was greatly excited by the idea of this wondrous chasm), "all the blood that the Romans shed, whether on battle-fields, or in the Coliseum, or on the cross—in whatever public or private murder—ran into this fatal gulf, and formed a mighty subterranean lake of gore, right beneath our feet. The blood from the thirty wounds in Cæsar's breast flowed hitherward, and that pure little rivulet from Virginia's bosom, too! Virginia, beyond all question, was stabbed by her father, precisely where we are standing."

"Then the spot is hallowed for ever!" said Hilda.

"Is there such blessed potency in bloodshed?" asked Miriam. "Nay, Hilda, do not protest! I take your meaning rightly."

They again moved forward. And still, from the Forum and the Via Sacra, from beneath the arches of the Temple of Peace on one side, and the acclivity of the Palace of the Cæsars on the other, there arose singing voices of parties that were strolling through the moonlight. Thus, the air was full of kindred melodies that encountered one another, and twined themselves into a broad, vague music, out of which no single strain could be disentangled. These good examples, as well as the harmonious influences of the hour, incited our artist-friends to make proof of their own vocal powers. With what skill and breath they had, they set up a choral strain—"Hail, Columbia!" we believe—which those old Roman echoes must have found it exceeding difficult to repeat aright. Even Hilda poured the slender sweetness of her note into her country's song. Miriam was at first silent, being perhaps unfamiliar with the air and burden. But, suddenly, she threw out such a swell and gush of sound, that it seemed to pervade the whole choir of other voices, and then to rise above them all, and become audible in what would else have been the silence of an upper region. That volume of melodious voice was one of the tokens of a great trouble. There had long been an impulse upon her—amounting, at last, to a necessity—to shriek aloud; but she had struggled against it, till the thunderous anthem gave her an opportunity to relieve her heart by a great cry.

They passed the solitary column of Phocas, and looked down into the excavated space, where a confusion of pillars, arches, pavements, and shattered blocks and shafts—the crumbs of various ruin, dropt from the devouring maw of Time— stand, or lie, at the base of the Capitoline Hill. That renowned hillock (for it is little more) now rose abruptly above them. The ponderous masonry, with which the hill-side is built up, is as old as Rome itself, and looks likely to endure, while the world retains any substance or permanence. It once sustained the Capitol, and now bears up the great pile which the mediæval builders raised on the antique foundation, and that still loftier tower, which looks abroad upon a larger page, of deeper historic interest, than any other scene can show. On the same pedestal of Roman masonry, other structures will doubtless rise, and vanish like ephemeral things.

To a spectator on the spot, it is remarkable that the events of Roman history, and Roman life itself, appear not so distant as the Gothic ages which succeeded them. We stand in the Forum, or on the height of the Capitol, and seem to see the Roman epoch close at hand. We forget that a chasm extends between it and ourselves, in which lie all those dark, rude, unlettered centuries, around the birth-time of Christianity, as well as the age of chivalry and romance, the feudal system, and the infancy of a better civilization than that of Rome. Or, if we remember these mediæval times, they look farther off than the Augustan age. The reason may be, that the old Roman literature survives, and creates for us an intimacy with the classic ages, which we have no means of forming with the subsequent ones.

The Italian climate, moreover, robs age of its reverence, and makes it look newer than it is. Not the Coliseum, nor the tombs of the Appian Way, nor the oldest pillar in the Forum, nor any other Roman ruin, be it as dilapidated as it may, ever give the impression of venerable antiquity which we gather, along with the ivy, from the gray walls of an English abbey or castle. And yet every brick or stone, which we pick up among the former, had fallen, ages before the foundation of the latter was begun. This is owing to the kindliness with which Nature takes an English ruin to her heart, covering it with ivy, as tenderly as Robin Redbreast covered the dead babes with forest leaves. She strives to make it a part of herself, gradually obliterating

the handiwork of man, and supplanting it with
her own mosses and trailing verdure, till she has
won the whole structure back. But, in Italy,
whenever man has once hewn a stone, Nature
forthwith relinquishes her right to it, and never
lays her finger on it again. Age after age finds
it bare and naked, in the barren sunshine, and
leaves it so. Besides this natural disadvantage,
too, each succeeding century, in Rome, has done
its best to ruin the very ruins, so far as their
picturesque effect is concerned, by stealing away
the marble and hewn stone, and leaving only
yellow bricks, which never can look venerable.

The party ascended the winding way that leads
from the Forum to the Piazza of the Campidoglio,
on the summit of the Capitoline Hill. They
stood awhile to contemplate the bronze equestrian
statue of Marcus Aurelius. The moonlight glis-
tened upon traces of the gilding which had once
covered both rider and steed; these were almost
gone, but the aspect of dignity was still perfect,
clothing the figure as it were with an imperial

robe of light. It is the most majestic representation of the kingly character that ever the world has seen. A sight of the old heathen Emperor is enough to create an evanescent sentiment of loyalty even in a democratic bosom, so august does he look, so fit to rule, so worthy of man's profoundest homage and obedience, so inevitably attractive of his love. He stretches forth his hand with an air of grand beneficence and unlimited authority, as if uttering a decree from which no appeal was permissible, but in which the obedient subject would find his highest interests consulted; a command that was in itself a benediction.

"The sculptor of this statue knew what a king should be," observed Kenyon, "and knew, likewise, the heart of mankind, and how it craves a true ruler, under whatever title, as a child its father."

"Oh, if there were but one such man as this!" exclaimed Miriam. "One such man in an age, and one in all the world; then how speedily would the strife, wickedness, and sorrow of us poor creatures be relieved. We would come to him with our griefs, whatever they might be—even a poor, frail woman burdened with her heavy heart—and lay them at his feet, and never need to take them up again. The rightful king would see to all."

"What an idea of the regal office and duty!" said Kenyon, with a smile. "It is a woman's idea of the whole matter, to perfection. It is Hilda's too, no doubt?"

"No," answered the quiet Hilda; "I should never look for such assistance from an earthly king."

"Hilda, my religious Hilda," whispered Miriam, suddenly drawing the girl close to her, "do you know how it is with me? I would give all I have or hope—my life, oh, how freely—for one instant of your trust in God! You little guess my need of it. You really think, then, that He sees and cares for us?"

"Miriam, you frighten me."

"Hush, hush! do not let them hear you!" whispered Miriam. "I frighten you, you say?

for Heaven's sake, how? Am I strange? is there anything wild in my behaviour?"

"Only for that moment," replied Hilda, "because you seemed to doubt God's providence."

"We will talk of that another time," said her friend. "Just now it is very dark to me."

On the left of the Piazza of the Campidoglio, as you face cityward, and at the head of the long and stately flight of steps descending from the Capitoline Hill to the level of lower Rome, there is a narrow lane or passage. Into this the party of our friends now turned. The path ascended a little and ran along under the walls of a palace, but soon passed through a gateway, and terminated in a small paved courtyard. It was bordered by a low parapet.

The spot, for some reason or other, impressed them as exceedingly lonely. On one side was the great height of the palace, with the moonshine falling over it, and showing all the windows barred and shuttered. Not a human eye could look down into the little courtyard, even if the seemingly deserted palace had a tenant. On all other sides of its narrow compass, there was nothing but the parapet, which as it now appeared was built right on the edge of a steep precipice. Gazing from its imminent brow, the party beheld a crowded confusion of roofs, spreading over the whole space between them and the line of hills that lay beyond the Tiber. A long, misty wreath, just dense enough to catch a little of the moonshine, floated above the houses midway towards the hilly line, and showed the course of the unseen river. Far away on the right, the moon gleamed on the dome of St. Peter's as well as on many lesser and nearer domes.

"What a beautiful view of the city!" exclaimed Hilda; "and I never saw Rome from this point before."

"It ought to afford a good prospect," said the sculptor; "for it was from this point—at least, we are at liberty to think so, if we choose—that many a famous Roman caught his last glimpse of his native city, and of all other earthly things.

This is one of the sides of the Tarpeian Rock. Look over the parapet and see what a sheer tumble there might still be for a traitor, in spite of the thirty feet of soil that have accumulated at the foot of the precipice.

They all bent over, and saw that the cliff fell perpendicularly downward to about the depth, or rather more, at which the tall palace rose in height above their heads. Not that it was still the natural, shaggy front of the original precipice; for it appeared to be cased in ancient stone-work, through which the primeval rock showed its face here and there grimly and doubtfully. Mosses grew on the slight projections, and little shrubs sprouted out of the crevices, but could not much soften the stern aspect of the cliff. Brightly as the Italian moonlight fell a-down the height, it scarcely showed what portion of it was man's work, and what was Nature's, but left it all in very much the same kind of ambiguity and half-knowledge in which antiquarians generally leave the identity of Roman remains.

The roofs of some poor-looking houses which had been built against the base and sides of the cliff, rose nearly midway to the top; but from an angle of the parapet there was a precipitous plunge straight downward into a stone-paved court.

"I prefer this to any other site as having been veritably the Traitor's Leap," said Kenyon, "because it was so convenient to the Capitol. It was an admirable idea of those stern old fellows, to fling their political criminals down from the very summit on which stood the Senate House and Jove's temple, emblems of the institutions which they sought to violate. It symbolizes how sudden was the fall in those days, from the utmost height of ambition to its profoundest ruin."

"Come, come; it is midnight," cried another artist, "too late to be moralizing here. We are literary dreaming on the edge of a precipice. Let us go home."

"It is time, indeed," said Hilda.

The sculptor was not without hopes that he

might be favoured with the sweet charge of
escorting Hilda to the foot of her tower. Accordingly, when the party prepared to turn back,
he offered her his arm. Hilda at first accepted
it; but when they had partly threaded the passage between the little courtyard and the Piazza
del Campidoglio, she discovered that Miriam had
remained behind.

"I must go back," said she, withdrawing her
arm from Kenyon's; "but pray do not come
with me. Several times this evening I have had
a fancy that Miriam had something on her mind,
some sorrow or perplexity, which, perhaps, it
would relieve her to tell me about. No, no;
do not turn back! Donatello will be a sufficient
guardian for Miriam and me."

The sculptor was a good deal mortified, and
perhaps a little angry; but he knew Hilda's
mood of gentle decision and independence too
well not to obey her. He therefore suffered the
fearless maiden to return alone.

Meanwhile, Miriam had not noticed the departure of the rest of the company; she remained on the edge of the precipice, and Donatello along with her.

"It would be a fatal fall, still," she said to herself, looking over the parapet, and shuddering as her eye measured the depth. "Yes; surely, yes! Even without the weight of an over-burdened heart, a human body would fall heavily enough upon those stones to shake all its joints asunder. How soon it would be over!"

Donatello, of whose presence she was possibly not aware, now pressed closer to her side; and he, too, like Miriam, bent over the low parapet and trembled violently. Yet he seemed to feel that perilous fascination which haunts the brow of precipices, tempting the unwary one to fling himself over, for the very horror of the thing, for, after drawing hastily back, he again looked down, thrusting himself out farther than before. He then stood silent a brief space, struggling, perhaps, to make himself conscious of the historic associations of the scene.

"What are you thinking of, Donatello?" asked Miriam.

"Who were they," said he, looking earnestly in her face, "who have been flung over here in days gone by?"

"Men that cumbered the world," she replied. "Men whose lives were the bane of their fellow-creatures. Men who poisoned the air, which is the common breath of all, for their own selfish purposes. There was short work with such men in old Roman times. Just in the moment of their triumph, a hand, as of an avenging giant, clutched them, and dashed the wretches down this precipice."

"Was it well done?" asked the young man.

"It was well done," answered Miriam; "innocent persons were saved by the destruction of a guilty one, who deserved his doom."

While this brief conversation passed, Donatello had once or twice glanced aside with a watchful air, just as a hound may often be seen to take sidelong note of some suspicious object, while he

gives his more direct attention to something
nearer at hand. Miriam seemed now first to
become aware of the silence that had followed
upon the cheerful talk and laughter of a few
moments before. Looking round, she perceived
that all her company of merry friends had retired, and Hilda, too, in whose soft and quiet
presence she had always an indescribable feeling of security. All gone; and only herself and
Donatello left hanging over the brow of the
ominous precipice.

Not so, however; not entirely alone! In the
basement wall of the palace, shaded from the
moon, there was a deep, empty niche, that had
probably once contained a statue; not empty,
either; for a figure now came forth from it,
and approached Miriam. She must have had
cause to dread some unspeakable evil from this
strange persecutor, and to know that this was
the very crisis of her calamity; for, as he drew
near, such a cold, sick despair crept over her,
that it impeded her breath, and benumbed her

natural promptitude of thought. Miriam seemed dreamily to remember falling on her knees; but, in her whole recollection of that wild moment, she beheld herself as in a dim show, and could not well distinguish what was done and suffered; no, not even whether she were really an actor and sufferer in the scene.

Hilda, meanwhile, had separated herself from the sculptor, and turned back to rejoin her friend. At a distance, she still heard the mirth of her late companions, who were going down the cityward descent of the Capitoline Hill; they had set up a new stave of melody, in which her own soft voice, as well as the powerful sweetness of Miriam's, was sadly missed.

The door of the little courtyard had swung upon its hinges, and partly closed itself. Hilda (whose native gentleness pervaded all her movements) was quietly opening it, when she was startled, midway, by the noise of a struggle within, beginning and ending all in one breathless instant. Along with it, or closely succeeding it, was a loud, fearful cry, which quivered upward through the air, and sank quivering downward to the earth. Then, a silence! Poor Hilda had looked into the courtyard, and saw the whole quick passage of a deed, which took but that little time to grave itself in the eternal adamant.

CHAPTER III.

THE FAUN'S TRANSFORMATION.

THE door of the courtyard swang slowly, and closed itself of its own accord. Miriam and Donatello were now alone there. She clasped her hands, and looked wildly at the young man, whose form seemed to have dilated, and whose eyes blazed with the fierce energy that had suddenly inspired him. It had kindled him into a man; it had developed within him an intelligence which was no native characteristic of the Donatello whom we have heretofore known. But that simple and joyous creature was gone for ever.

"What have you done?" said Miriam, in a horror-stricken whisper.

The glow of rage was still lurid on Donatello's face, and now flashed out again from his eyes.

"I did what ought to be done to a traitor!" he replied. "I did what your eyes bade me do, when I asked them with mine, as I held the wretch over the precipice!"

These last words struck Miriam like a bullet. Could it be so? Had her eyes provoked, or assented to this deed? She had not known it. But, alas! looking back into the frenzy and turmoil of the scene just acted, she could not deny—she was not sure whether it might be so, or no—that a wild joy had flamed up in her heart, when she beheld her persecutor in his mortal peril. Was it horror?—or ecstasy?—or both in one? Be the emotion what it might, it had blazed up more madly, when Donatello flung his victim off the cliff, and more and more, while his shriek went quivering downward. With the dead thump upon the stones below, had come an unutterable horror.

"And my eyes bade you do it!" repeated she.

They both leaned over the parapet, and gazed

downward as earnestly as if some inestimable treasure had fallen over, and were yet recoverable. On the pavement, below, was a dark mass, lying in a heap, with little or nothing human in its appearance, except that the hands were stretched out, as if they might have clutched, for a moment, at the small square stones. But there was no motion in them, now. Miriam watched the heap of mortality while she could count a hundred, which she took pains to do. No stir; not a finger moved.

"You have killed him, Donatello! He is quite dead!" said she. "Stone dead! Would I were so, too!"

"Did you not mean that he should die?" sternly asked Donatello, still in the glow of that intelligence which passion had developed in him. "There was short time to weigh the matter; but he had his trial in that breath or two, while I held him over the cliff, and his sentence in that one glance, when your eyes responded to mine! Say that I have slain him against your will—say that he died without your whole consent—and, in another breath, you shall see me lying beside him."

"Oh, never!" cried Miriam. "My one, own friend! Never, never, never!"

She turned to him—the guilty, blood-stained, lonely woman—she turned to her fellow-criminal, the youth; so lately innocent, whom she had drawn into her doom. She pressed him close, close to her bosom, with a clinging embrace that brought their two hearts together, till the horror and agony of each was combined into one emotion, and that, a kind of rapture.

"Yes, Donatello, you speak the truth!" said she; "my heart consented to what you did. We two slew yonder wretch. The deed knots us together for time and eternity, like the coil of a serpent!"

They threw one other glance at the heap of death below, to assure themselves that it was there; so like a dream was the whole thing. Then they turned from that fatal precipice, and came out of the courtyard, arm in arm, heart in heart. Instinctively, they were heedful not to sever themselves so much as a pace or two from one another, for fear of the terror and deadly chill that would thenceforth wait for them in solitude. Their deed—the crime which Donatello wrought, and Miriam accepted on the instant—had wreathed itself, as she said, like a serpent, in inextricable links about both their souls, and drew them into one, by its terrible contractile power. It was closer than a marriage-bond. So intimate, in those first moments, was the union that it seemed as if their new sympathy annihilated all other ties, and that they were released from the chain of humanity; a new sphere, a special law, had been created for them alone. The world could not come near them; they were safe!

When they reached the flight of steps, leading downward from the Capitol, there was a far-off noise of singing and laughter. Swift, indeed, had been the rush of the crisis that was come and gone! This was still the merriment of the party that had so recently been their companions; they recognized the voices which, a little while ago, had accorded and sung in cadence with their own. But they were familiar voices no more; they sounded strangely, and, as it were, out of the depths of space; so remote was all that pertained to the past life of these guilty ones, in the moral seclusion that had suddenly extended itself around them. But how close, and ever closer, did the breadth of the immeasurable waste, that lay between them and all brotherhood or sisterhood, now press them one within the other!

"Oh, friend," cried Miriam, so putting her soul into that word that it took a heavy richness of meaning, and seemed never to have been spoken before. "Oh, friend, are you conscious, as I am, of this companionship that knits our heart-strings together?"

"I feel it, Miriam," said Donatello. "We draw one breath; we live one life!"

THE FAUN'S TRANSFORMATION.

"Only yesterday," continued Miriam; "nay, only a short half-hour ago, I shivered in an icy solitude. No friendship, no sisterhood, could come near enough to keep the warmth within my heart. In an instant, all is changed! There can be no more loneliness!"

"None, Miriam!" said Donatello.

"None, my beautiful one!" responded Miriam, gazing in his face, which had taken a higher, almost an heroic aspect from the strength of passion. "None, my innocent one! Surely, it is no crime that we have committed. One wretched and worthless life has been sacrificed, to cement two other lives for evermore."

"For evermore, Miriam!" said Donatello; "cemented with his blood!"

The young man started at the word which he had himself spoken; it may be that it brought home, to the simplicity of his imagination, what he had not before dreamed of—the ever-increasing loathsomeness of a union that consists in guilt. Cemented with blood, which would corrupt and

grow more noisome for ever and for ever, but
bind them none the less strictly for that!

"Forget it! Cast it all behind you!" said
Miriam, detecting, by her sympathy, the pang
that was in his heart. "The deed has done its
office, and has no existence any more."

They flung the past behind them, as she counselled, or else distilled from it a fiery intoxication,
which sufficed to carry them triumphantly through
those first moments of their doom. For, guilt
has its moment of rapture, too. The foremost
result of a broken law is ever an ecstatic sense
of freedom. And thus there exhaled upward
(out of their dark sympathy, at the base of
which lay a human corpse) a bliss, or an insanity,
which the unhappy pair imagined to be well worth
the sleepy innocence that was for ever lost to
them.

As their spirits rose to the solemn madness of
the occasion, they went onward—not stealthily,
not fearfully—but with a stately gait and aspect.
Passion lent them (as it does to meaner shapes)

its brief nobility of carriage. They trode through the streets of Rome, as if they, too, were among the majestic and guilty shadows, that, from ages long gone by, have haunted the blood-stained city. And, at Miriam's suggestion, they turned aside, for the sake of treading loftily past the old site of Pompey's forum.

"For there was a great deed done here!" she said—"a deed of blood, like ours! Who knows, but we may meet the high and ever-sad fraternity of Cæsar's murderers, and exchange a salutation?"

"Are they our brethren, now?" asked Donatello.

"Yes; all of them," said Miriam; "and many another, whom the world little dreams of, has been made our brother or our sister, by what we have done within this hour!"

And, at the thought, she shivered. Where, then, was the seclusion, the remoteness, the strange, lonesome Paradise, into which she and her one companion had been transported by their crime? Was there, indeed, no such refuge, but only a crowded thoroughfare and jostling throng of criminals? And was it true, that whatever hand had a blood-stain on it—or had poured out poison—or strangled a babe at its birth—or clutched a grandsire's throat, he sleeping, and robbed him of his few last breaths—had now the right to offer itself in fellowship with their two hands? Too certainly, that right existed. It is a terrible thought, that an individual wrong-doing melts into the great mass of human crime, and makes us—who dreamed only of our own little separate sin—makes us guilty of the whole. And thus Miriam and her lover were not an insulated pair, but members of an innumerable confraternity of guilty ones, all shuddering at each other.

"But not now; not yet," she murmured to herself. "To-night, at least, there shall be no remorse!"

Wandering without a purpose, it so chanced that they turned into a street, at one extremity of which stood Hilda's tower. There was a light in her high chamber; a light, too, at the Virgin's shrine; and the glimmer of these two was the loftiest light beneath the stars. Miriam drew Donatello's arm to make him stop, and while they stood at some distance looking at Hilda's window, they beheld her approach and throw it open. She leaned far forth, and extended her clasped hands towards the sky.

"The good, pure child! She is praying, Donatello," said Miriam, with a kind of simple joy at witnessing the devoutness of her friend. Then her own sin rushed upon her, and she shouted, with the rich strength of her voice, "Pray for us, Hilda; we need it!"

Whether Hilda heard and recognized the voice, we cannot tell. The window was immediately closed, and her form disappeared from behind the snowy curtain. Miriam felt this to be a token that the cry of her condemned spirit was shut out of heaven.

CHAPTER IV.

THE BURIAL CHAUNT.

THE Church of the Capuchins (where, as the reader may remember, some of our acquaintances had made an engagement to meet) stands a little aside from the Piazza Barberini. Thither, at the hour agreed upon on the morning after the scenes last described, Miriam and Donatello directed their steps. At no time are people so sedulously careful to keep their trifling appointments, attend to their ordinary occupations, and thus put a commonplace aspect on life, as when conscious of some secret that if suspected would make them look monstrous in the general eye.

Yet how tame and wearisome is the impression of all ordinary things in the contrast with such a fact! How sick and tremulous, the next morning, is the spirit that has dared so much, only the night before! How icy cold is the heart, when the fervour, the wild ecstasy of passion has faded away, and sunk down among the dead ashes of the fire that blazed so fiercely, and was fed by the very substance of its life! How faintly does the criminal stagger onward, lacking the impulse of that strong madness that hurried him into guilt, and treacherously deserts him in the midst of it!

When Miriam and Donatello drew near the church, they found only Kenyon awaiting them on the steps. Hilda had likewise promised to be of the party, but had not yet appeared. Meeting the sculptor, Miriam put a force upon herself and succeeded in creating an artificial flow of spirits, which, to any but the nicest observation, was quite as effective as a natural one. She spoke sympathizingly to the sculptor on the subject of Hilda's absence, and somewhat annoyed him by alluding, in Donatello's hearing, to an attachment which had never been openly avowed, though perhaps plainly enough betrayed. He fancied that Miriam did not quite recognize the limits of the strictest delicacy; he even went so far as to generalize, and conclude within himself that this deficiency is a more general failing in woman than in man, the highest refinement being a masculine attribute.

But the idea was unjust to the sex at large, and especially so to this poor Miriam, who was hardly responsible for her frantic efforts to be gay. Possibly, moreover, the nice action of the mind is set ajar by any violent shock, as of great misfortune or great crime, so that the finer perceptions may be blurred thenceforth, and the effect be traceable in all the minutest conduct of life.

"Did you see anything of the dear child after you left us?" asked Miriam, still keeping Hilda as her topic of conversation. "I missed her sadly on my way homeward; for nothing ensures me such delightful and innocent dreams (I have experienced it twenty times) as a talk late in the evening with Hilda."

"So I should imagine," said the sculptor, gravely; "but it is an advantage that I have little or no opportunity of enjoying. I know not what became of Hilda after my parting from you. She was not especially my companion in any part of our walk. The last I saw of her, she was hastening back to rejoin you in the court-yard of the Palazzo Caffarelli."

"Impossible!" cried Miriam, starting.

"Then did you not see her again?" inquired Kenyon, in some alarm.

"Not there," answered Miriam, quietly; "indeed, I followed pretty closely on the heels of the rest of the party. But do not be alarmed on Hilda's account: the Virgin is bound to watch over the good child, for the sake of the piety with which she keeps the lamp alight at her shrine. And, besides, I have always felt that Hilda is just as safe in these evil streets of Rome, as her white doves when they fly downward from the tower-top, and run to and fro among the horses' feet. There is certainly a providence or purpose for Hilda, if for no other human creature."

"I religiously believe it," rejoined the sculptor; "and yet my mind would be the easier, if I knew that she had returned safely to her tower."

"Then make yourself quite easy," answered Miriam. "I saw her (and it is the last sweet sight that I remember) leaning from her window midway between earth and sky!"

Kenyon now looked at Donatello.

"You seem out of spirits, my dear friend," he observed. "This languid Roman atmosphere is not the airy wine that you were accustomed to breathe at home. I have not forgotten your hospitable invitation to meet you this summer at your castle among the Apennines. It is my fixed purpose to come, I assure you. We shall both be the better for some deep draughts of the mountain-breezes."

"It may be," said Donatello, with unwonted sombreness; "the old house seemed joyous when

I was a child. But as I remember it now, it was a grim place, too."

The sculptor looked more attentively at the young man, and was surprised and alarmed to observe how entirely the fine, fresh glow of animal spirits had departed out of his face. Hitherto, moreover, even while he was standing perfectly still, there had been a kind of possible gambol indicated in his aspect. It was quite gone now. All his youthful gaiety, and with it his simplicity of manner, was eclipsed, if not utterly extinct.

"You are surely ill, my dear fellow," exclaimed Kenyon.

"Am I? Perhaps so," said Donatello, indifferently, "I never have been ill, and know not what it may be."

"Do not make the poor lad fancy-sick," whispered Miriam, pulling the sculptor's sleeve. "He is of a nature to lie down and die at once, if he finds himself drawing such melancholy breaths as we ordinary people are enforced to burden our lungs withal. But we must get him away from this old, dreamy, and dreary Rome, where nobody but himself ever thought of being gay. Its influences are too heavy to sustain the life of such a creature."

The above conversation had passed chiefly on the steps of the Cappuccini; and, having said so much, Miriam lifted the leathern curtain that hangs before all church doors in Italy.

"Hilda has forgotten her appointment," she observed, "or else her maiden slumbers are very sound this morning. We will wait for her no longer."

They entered the nave. The interior of the church was of moderate compass, but of good architecture, with a vaulted roof over the nave, and a row of dusky chapels on either side of it, instead of the customary side-aisles. Each chapel had its saintly shrine, hung round with offerings; its picture above the altar, although closely veiled, if by any painter of renown; and its hallowed tapers, burning continually, to set alight the devotion of the worshippers. The pavement of the nave was chiefly of marble, and looked old and broken, and was shabbily patched here and there with tiles of brick; it was inlaid, moreover, with tombstones of the mediæval taste, on which were quaintly sculptured borders, figures, and portraits in bas-relief, and Latin epitaphs, now grown illegible by the tread of footsteps over them. The church appertains to a convent of Capuchin monks; and, as usually happens when a reverend brotherhood have such an edifice in charge, the floor seemed never to have been scrubbed or swept, and had as little the aspect of sanctity as a kennel; whereas, in all churches of nunneries, the maiden sisterhood invariably show the purity of their own hearts by the virgin cleanliness and visible consecration of the walls and pavement.

As our friends entered the church, their eyes rested at once on a remarkable object in the centre of the nave. It was either the actual

body; or, as might rather have been supposed
at first glance, the cunningly wrought waxen
face and suitably draped figure of a dead monk.
This image of wax or clay-cold reality, which-
ever it might be, lay on a slightly elevated
bier, with three tall candles burning on each
side, another tall candle at the head, and another at the foot. There was music, too, in
harmony with so funereal a spectacle. From beneath the pavement of the church came the
deep, lugubrious strain of a *De Profundis*,
which sounded like an utterance of the tomb
itself; so dismally did it rumble through the
burial-vaults, and ooze up among the flat grave-
stones and sad epitaphs, filling the church as
with a gloomy mist.

"I must look more closely at that dead monk
before we leave the church," remarked the sculptor. "In the study of my art, I have gained
many a hint from the dead, which the living
could never have given me."

"I can well imagine it," answered Miriam,

"One clay image is readily copied from another. But let us first see Guido's picture. The light is favourable now."

Accordingly, they turned into the first chapel on the right hand, as you enter the nave; and there they beheld—not the picture, indeed—but a closely drawn curtain. The churchmen of Italy make no scruple of sacrificing the very purpose for which a work of sacred art has been created; that of opening the way for religious sentiment through the quick medium of sight, by bringing angels, saints, and martyrs, down visibly upon earth; of sacrificing this high purpose, and, for aught they know, the welfare of many souls along with it, to the hope of a paltry fee. Every work by an artist of celebrity, is hidden behind a veil, and seldom revealed, except to Protestants, who scorn it as an object of devotion, and value it only for its artistic merit.

The sacristan was quickly found, however, and lost no time in disclosing the youthful Archangel, setting his divine foot on the head of his fallen adversary. It was an image of that greatest of future events, which we hope for so ardently, at least, while we are young, but find so very long in coming—the triumph of goodness over the evil principle.

"Where can Hilda be?" exclaimed Kenyon. "It is not her custom ever to fail in an engagement; and the present one was made entirely on her account. Except herself, you know, we were all agreed in our recollection of the picture."

"But we were wrong, and Hilda right, as you perceive," said Miriam, directing his attention to the point on which their dispute of the night before had arisen. "It is not easy to detect her astray, as regards any picture on which those clear, soft eyes of hers have ever rested."

"And she has studied and admired few pictures so much as this," observed the sculptor. "No wonder; for there is hardly another so beautiful in the world. What an expression of heavenly severity in the Archangel's face! There is a degree of pain, trouble, and disgust at being brought in contact with sin, even for the purpose of quelling and punishing it; and yet a celestial tranquillity pervades his whole being."

"I have never been able," said Miriam, "to admire this picture nearly so much as Hilda does, in its moral and intellectual aspect. If it cost her more trouble to be good, if her soul were less white and pure, she would be a more competent critic of this picture, and would estimate it not half so high. I see its defects to-day more clearly than ever before."

"What are some of them?" asked Kenyon.

"That Archangel, now," Miriam continued, "how fair he looks, with his unruffled wings, with his unhacked sword, and clad in his bright armour, and that exquisitely fitting sky-blue tunic, cut in the latest Paradisaical mode! What a dainty air of the first celestial society! With what half-scornful delicacy he sets his prettily

sandalled foot on the head of his prostrate foe!
But, is it thus that virtue looks, the moment
after its death-struggle with evil? No, no; I
could have told Guido better. A full third
of the Archangel's feathers should have been
torn from his wings; the rest all ruffled, till
they looked like Satan's own! His sword should
be streaming with blood, and perhaps broken
half way to the hilt; his armour crushed, his
robes rent, his breast gory; a bleeding gash on
his brow, cutting right across the stern scowl
of battle! He should press his foot hard down
upon the old serpent, as if his very soul de-
pended upon it, feeling him squirm mightily,
and doubting whether the fight were half over
yet, and how the victory might turn! And,
with all this fierceness, this grimness, this unutterable horror, there should still be something
high, tender, and holy, in Michael's eyes, and
around his mouth. But the battle never was
such child's play as Guido's dapper Archangel
seems to have found it."

"For Heaven's sake, Miriam," cried Kenyon, astonished at the wild energy of her talk; "paint the picture of man's struggle against sin according to your own idea! I think it will be a masterpiece."

"The picture would have its share of truth, I assure you," she answered; "but I am sadly afraid the victory would fall on the wrong side. Just fancy a smoke-blackened, fiery-eyed demon, bestriding that nice young angel, clutching his white throat with one of his hinder claws, and giving a triumphant whisk of his scaly tail, with a poisonous dart at the end of it! That is what they risk, poor souls, who do battle with Michael's enemy."

It now, perhaps, struck Miriam that her mental disquietude was impelling her to an undue vivacity; for she paused, and turned away from the picture, without saying a word more about it. All this while, moreover, Donatello had been very ill at ease, casting awe-stricken and inquiring glances at the dead monk; as if he could look nowhere but at that ghastly object, merely because it shocked him. Death has probably a peculiar horror and ugliness, when forced upon the contemplation of a person so naturally joyous as Donatello, who lived with completeness in the present moment, and was able to form but vague images of the future.

"What is the matter, Donatello?" whispered Miriam soothingly. "You are quite in a tremble, my poor friend! What is it?"

"This awful chaunt from beneath the church," answered Donatello, "it oppresses me; the air is so heavy with it that I can scarcely draw my breath. And yonder dead monk! I feel as if he were lying right across my heart."

"Take courage!" whispered she again, "come; we will approach close to the dead monk. The only way, in such cases, is to stare the ugly horror right in the face; never a side-long glance, nor a half-look, for those are what show a frightful thing in its frightfulest aspect. Lean on me, dearest friend! My heart is very strong for both of us. Be brave; and all is well."

Donatello hung back for a moment, but then pressed close to Miriam's side, and suffered her to lead him up to the bier. The sculptor followed. A number of persons, chiefly women, with several children among them, were standing about the corpse; and as our three friends drew nigh, a mother knelt down, and caused her little boy to kneel, both kissing the beads and crucifix that hung from the monk's girdle. Possibly he had died in the odour of sanctity; or, at all events, death and his brown frock and cowl made a sacred image of this reverend father.

CHAPTER V.

THE DEAD CAPUCHIN.

The dead monk was clad, as when alive, in the brown woollen frock of the Capuchins, with the hood drawn over his head, but so as to leave the features and a portion of the beard uncovered. His rosary and cross hung at his side; his hands were folded over his breast; his feet (he was of a bare-footed order, in his lifetime, and continued so in death) protruded from beneath his habit, stiff and stark, with a more waxen look than even his face. They were tied together at the ankles with a black ribbon.

The countenance, as we have already said, was fully displayed. It had a purplish hue upon it, unlike the paleness of an ordinary corpse, but as little resembling the flush of natural life. The eyelids were but partially drawn down, and showed the eyeballs beneath; as if the deceased friar were stealing a glimpse at the bystanders, to watch whether they were duly impressed with the solemnity of his obsequies. The shaggy eyebrows gave sternness to the look.

Miriam passed between two of the lighted candles, and stood close beside the bier.

"My God!" murmured she. "What is this?"

She grasped Donatello's hand, and, at the same instant, felt him give a convulsive shudder, which she knew to have been caused by a sudden and terrible throb of the heart. His hand, by an instantaneous change, became like ice within hers, which likewise grew so icy, that their insensible fingers might have rattled, one against the other. No wonder that their blood curdled; no wonder that their hearts leapt, and paused! The dead face of the monk, gazing at them beneath its half-closed eyelids, was the same visage that had glared upon their naked souls, the past midnight, as Donatello flung him over the precipice.

The sculptor was standing at the foot of the bier, and had not yet seen the monk's features.

"Those naked feet!" said he. "I know not why, but they affect me strangely. They have walked to and fro over the hard pavements of Rome, and through a hundred other rough ways of this life, where the monk went begging for his brotherhood; along the cloisters and dreary corridors of his convent, too, from his youth upward! It is a suggestive idea, to track those worn feet backward through all the paths they have trodden, ever since they were the tender and rosy little feet of a baby, and (cold as they now are) were kept warm in his mother's hand."

As his companions, whom the sculptor supposed to be close by him, made no response to his fanciful musing, he looked up, and saw them at the head of the bier. He advanced thither himself.

"Ha!" exclaimed he.

He cast a horror-stricken and bewildered glance at Miriam, but withdrew it immediately. Not that he had any definite suspicion, or, it may be, even a remote idea, that she could be held responsible, in the least degree, for this man's sudden death. In truth, it seemed too wild a thought, to connect, in reality, Miriam's persecutor of many past months, and the vagabond of the preceding night, with the dead Capuchin of to-day. It resembled one of those unaccountable changes and interminglings of identity, which so often occur among the personages of a dream. But Kenyon, as befitted the professor of an imaginative art, was endowed with an exceedingly quick sensibility, which was apt to give him intimations of the true state of matters that lay beyond his actual vision. There was a whisper in his ear; it said, "Hush!" Without asking himself wherefore, he resolved to be silent as regarded the mysterious discovery which he had made, and to leave any remark or explanation to be voluntarily offered by

Miriam. If she never spoke, then let the riddle be unsolved.

And now occurred a circumstance that would seem too fantastic to be told, if it had not actually happened, precisely as we set it down. As the three friends stood by the bier, they saw that a little stream of blood had begun to ooze from the dead monk's nostrils; it crept slowly towards the thicket of his beard, where, in the course of a moment or two, it hid itself.

"How strange!" ejaculated Kenyon. "The monk died of apoplexy, I suppose, or by some sudden accident, and the blood has not yet congealed."

"Do you consider that a sufficient explanation?" asked Miriam, with a smile from which the sculptor involuntarily turned away his eyes. "Does it satisfy you?"

"And why not?" he inquired.

"Of course, you know the old superstition about this phenomenon of blood flowing from a dead body," she rejoined. "How can we tell but that the murderer of this monk (or, possibly, it may be only that privileged murderer, his physician) may have just entered the church?"

"I cannot jest about it," said Kenyon. "It is an ugly sight!"

"True, true; horrible to see, or dream of!" she replied, with one of those long, tremulous sighs, which so often betray a sick heart by escaping unexpectedly. "We will not look at it any more. Come away, Donatello. Let us escape from this dismal church. The sunshine will do you good."

When had ever a woman such a trial to sustain as this! By no possible supposition could Miriam explain the identity of the dead Capuchin, quietly and decorously laid out in the nave of his convent church, with that of her murdered persecutor, flung heedlessly at the foot of the precipice. The effect upon her imagination was as if a strange and unknown corpse had miraculously, while she was gazing at it, assumed the likeness of that face, so terrible henceforth in her remembrance. It was a symbol, perhaps, of the deadly iteration with which she was doomed to behold the image of her crime reflected back upon her, in a thousand ways, and converting the great, calm face of Nature, in the whole, and in its innumerable details, into a manifold reminiscence of that one dead visage.

No sooner had Miriam turned away from the bier, and gone a few steps, than she fancied the likeness altogether an illusion, which would vanish at a closer and colder view. She must look at it again, therefore, and at once; or else the grave would close over the face, and leave the awful fantasy that had connected itself therewith, fixed ineffaceably in her brain.

"Wait for me, one moment!" she said to her companions. "Only a moment!"

So she went back, and gazed once more at the corpse. Yes; these were the features that Miriam had known so well; this was the visage that she remembered from a far longer date than the most intimate of her friends suspected; this

form of clay had held the evil spirit which
blasted her sweet youth, and compelled her, as
it were, to stain her womanhood with crime.
But, whether it were the majesty of death, or
something originally noble and lofty in the
character of the dead, which the soul had
stamped upon the features, as it left them; so
it was that Miriam now quailed and shook, not
for the vulgar horror of the spectacle, but for
the severe, reproachful glance that seemed to
come from between those half-closed lids. True,
there had been nothing, in his lifetime, viler
than this man. She knew it; there was no
other fact within her consciousness that she felt
to be so certain; and yet, because her persecutor
found himself safe and irrefutable in death, he
frowned upon his victim, and threw back the
blame on her!

"Is it thou, indeed?" she murmured, under
her breath. "Then thou hast no right to scowl
upon me so! But art thou real, or a vision?"

She bent down over the dead monk, till one

of her rich curls brushed against his forehead. She touched one of his folded hands with her finger.

"It is he!" said Miriam. "There is the scar, that I know so well, on his brow. And it is no vision; he is palpable to my touch! I will question the fact no longer, but deal with it as I best can."

It was wonderful to see how the crisis developed in Miriam its own proper strength, and the faculty of sustaining the demands which it made upon her fortitude. She ceased to tremble; the beautiful woman gazed sternly at her dead enemy, endeavoring to meet and quell the look of accusation that he threw from between his half-closed eyelids.

"No; thou shalt not scowl me down!" said she. "Neither now, nor when we stand together at the judgment-seat. I fear not to meet thee there. Farewell, till that next encounter!"

Haughtily waving her hand, Miriam rejoined her friends, who were awaiting her at the door of the church. As they went out, the sacristan stopped them, and proposed to show the cemetery of the convent, where the deceased members of the fraternity are laid to rest in sacred earth, brought long ago from Jerusalem.

"And will yonder monk be buried there?" she asked.

"Brother Antonio?" exclaimed the sacristan. "Surely, our good brother will be put to bed there! His grave is already dug, and the last occupant has made room for him. Will you look at it, signorina?"

"I will!" said Miriam.

"Then excuse me," observed Kenyon; "for I shall leave you. One dead monk has more than sufficed me; and I am not bold enough to face the whole mortality of the convent."

It was easy to see, by Donatello's looks, that he, as well as the sculptor, would gladly have escaped a visit to the famous cemetery of the Cappuccini. But Miriam's nerves were strained to such a pitch, that she anticipated a certain

solace and absolute relief in passing from one
ghastly spectacle to another of long-accumulated
ugliness; and there was, besides, a singular sense
of duty which impelled her to look at the final
resting-place of the being whose fate had been
so disastrously involved with her own. She
therefore followed the sacristan's guidance, and
drew her companion along with her, whispering
encouragement as they went.

The cemetery is beneath the church, but
entirely above ground, and lighted by a row of
iron-grated windows without glass. A corridor
runs along beside these windows, and gives
access to three or four vaulted recesses, or
chapels, of considerable breadth and height, the
floor of which consists of the consecrated earth
of Jerusalem. It is smoothed decorously over
the deceased brethren of the convent, and is
kept quite free from grass or weeds, such as
would grow even in these gloomy recesses, if
pains were not bestowed to root them up. But,
as the cemetery is small, and it is a precious

privilege to sleep in holy ground, the brotherhood are immemorially accustomed, when one of their number dies, to take the longest-buried skeleton out of the oldest grave, and lay the new slumberer there instead. Thus, each of the good friars, in his turn, enjoys the luxury of a consecrated bed, attended with the slight drawback of being forced to get up long before daybreak, as it were, and make room for another lodger.

The arrangement of the unearthed skeletons is what makes the special interest of the cemetery. The arched and vaulted walls of the burial recesses are supported by massive pillars and pilasters made of thigh-bones and skulls; the whole material of the structure appears to be of a similar kind; and the knobs and embossed ornaments of this strange architecture are represented by the joints of the spine, and the more delicate tracery by the smaller bones of the human frame. The summits of the arches are adorned with entire skeletons, looking as if they were wrought most skilfully in bas-relief. There is no possibility of describing how ugly and grotesque is the effect, combined with a certain artistic merit, nor how much perverted ingenuity has been shown in this queer way; nor what a multitude of dead monks, through how many hundred years, must have contributed their bony framework to build up these great arches of mortality. On some of the skulls there are inscriptions, purporting that such a monk, who formerly made use of that particular head-piece, died on such a day and year; but vastly the greater number are piled up indistinguishably into the architectural design like the many deaths that make up the one glory of a victory.

In the side walls of the vaults are niches where skeleton monks sit or stand, clad in the brown habits that they wore in life, and labelled with their names and the dates of their decease. Their skulls (some quite bare, and others still covered with yellow skin, and hair that has known the earth-damps) look out from beneath their hoods, grinning hideously repulsive. One reverend father has his mouth wide open, as if he had died in the midst of a howl of terror and remorse, which perhaps is even now screeching through eternity. As a general thing, however, these frocked and hooded skeletons seem to take a more cheerful view of their position, and try with ghastly smiles to turn it into a jest. But the cemetery of the Capuchins is no place to nourish celestial hopes; the soul sinks forlorn and wretched under all this burden of dusty death; the holy earth from Jerusalem, so imbued is it with mortality, has grown as barren of the flowers of Paradise as it is of earthly weeds and grass. Thank Heaven for its blue sky; it needs a long, upward gaze to give us back our faith. Not here can we feel ourselves immortal, where the very altars in these chapels of horrible consecration are heaps of human bones.

Yet let us give the cemetery the praise that it deserves. There is no disagreeable scent, such as might have been expected from the decay of so many holy persons, in whatever odour of sanctity they may have taken their departure. The same number of living monks would not smell half so unexceptionably.

Miriam went gloomily along the corridor, from one vaulted Golgotha to another, until in the farthest recess she beheld an open grave.

"Is that for him who lies yonder in the nave?" she asked.

"Yes, signorina, this is to be the resting-place of brother Antonio, who came to his death last night," answered the sacristan; "and in yonder niche, you see, sits a brother who was buried thirty years ago, and has risen to give him place."

"It is not a satisfactory idea," observed Miriam, "that you poor friars cannot call even your graves permanently your own. You must lie down in them, methinks, with a nervous anticipation of being disturbed, like weary men who know that they shall be summoned out of bed at midnight. Is it not possible (if money were to be paid for the privilege) to leave brother Antonio

—if that be his name—in the occupancy of that narrow grave till the last trumpet sounds?"

"By no means, signorina; neither is it needful or desirable," answered the sacristan. "A quarter of a century's sleep in the sweet earth of Jerusalem is better than a thousand years in any other soil. Our brethren find good rest there. No ghost was ever known to steal out of this blessed cemetery."

"That is well," responded Miriam; "may he whom you now lay to sleep prove no exception to the rule!"

As they left the cemetery she put money into the sacristan's hand, to an amount that made his eyes open wide and glisten, and requested that it might be expended in masses for the repose of Father Antonio's soul.

CHAPTER VI.

THE MEDICI GARDENS.

"Donatello," said Miriam, anxiously, as they came through the Piazza Barberini, "what can I do for you, my beloved friend? You are shaking as with the cold fit of the Roman fever."

"Yes," said Donatello, "my heart shivers."

As soon as she could collect her thoughts, Miriam led the young man to the gardens of the Villa Medici, hoping that the quiet shade and sunshine of that delightful retreat would a little revive his spirits. The grounds are there laid out in the old fashion of straight paths, with borders of box, which form hedges of great height and density, and are shorn and trimmed to the evenness of a wall of stone, at the top and sides. There are green alleys, with long vistas, overshadowed by ilex-trees; and at each intersection of the paths, the visitor finds seats of lichen-covered stone to repose upon, and marble statues that look forlornly at him, regretful of their lost noses. In the more open portions of the garden, before the sculptured front of the villa, you see fountains and flower-beds, and, in their season, a profusion of roses, from which the genial sun of Italy distils a fragrance, to be scattered abroad by the no less genial breeze.

But Donatello drew no delight from these things. He walked onward in silent apathy, and looked at Miriam with strangely half-awakened and bewildered eyes, when she sought to bring his mind into sympathy with hers, and so relieve his heart of the burden that lay lumpishly upon it.

She made him sit down on a stone bench, where two embowered alleys crossed each other; so that they could discern the approach of any casual intruder, a long way down the path.

"My sweet friend," she said, taking one of his

passive hands in both of hers, "what can I say to comfort you?"

"Nothing!" replied Donatello, with sombre reserve. "Nothing will ever comfort me."

"I accept my own misery," continued Miriam; "my own guilt, if guilt it be—and, whether guilt or misery, I shall know how to deal with it. But you, dearest friend, that were the rarest creature in all this world, and seemed a being to whom sorrow could not cling—you, whom I half fancied to belong to a race that had vanished for ever, you only surviving, to show mankind how genial and how joyous life used to be, in some long-gone age—what had you to do with grief or crime?"

"They came to me as to other men," said Donatello, broodingly. "Doubtless I was born to them."

"No, no; they came with me," replied Miriam. "Mine is the responsibility! Alas! wherefore was I born? Why did we ever meet? Why did I not drive you from me, knowing—for my heart foreboded it—that the cloud in which I walked would likewise envelop you!"

Donatello stirred uneasily, with the irritable impatience that is often combined with a mood of leaden despondency. A brown lizard with two tails—a monster often engendered by the Roman sunshine—ran across his foot, and made him start. Then he sat silent awhile, and so did Miriam, trying to dissolve her whole heart into sympathy, and lavish it all upon him, were it only for a moment's cordial.

The young man lifted his hand to his breast, and, intentionally, as Miriam's hand was within his, he lifted that along with it.

"I have a great weight here!" said he.

The fancy struck Miriam (but she drove it resolutely down) that Donatello almost imperceptibly shuddered, while, in pressing his own hand against his heart, he pressed hers there too.

"Rest your heart on me, dearest one!" she resumed. "Let me bear all its weight; I am well

able to bear it; for I am a woman, and I love
you! I love you, Donatello! Is there no comfort
for you in this avowal? Look at me! Heretofore, you have found me pleasant to your sight.
Gaze into my eyes! Gaze into my soul! Search
as deeply as you may, you can never see half
the tenderness and devotion that I henceforth
cherish for you. All that I ask, is your acceptance of the utter self-sacrifice (but it shall be no
sacrifice, to my great love) with which I seek
to remedy the evil you have incurred for my
sake!"

All this fervour on Miriam's part; on Donatello's, a heavy silence.

"Oh, speak to me!" she exclaimed. "Only
promise me to be, by and by, a little happy!"

"Happy?" murmured Donatello. "Ah, never
again! never again!"

"Never? Ah, that is a terrible word to say
to me!" answered Miriam. "A terrible word
to let fall upon a woman's heart, when she loves
you, and is conscious of having caused your

misery! If you love me, Donatello, speak it not again. And surely you did love me?"

"I did," replied Donatello, gloomily and absently.

Miriam released the young man's hand, but suffered one of her own to lie close to his, and waited a moment to see whether he would make any effort to retain it. There was much depending upon that simple experiment.

With a deep sigh—as when, sometimes, a slumberer turns over in a troubled dream—Donatello changed his position, and clasped both his hands over his forehead. The genial warmth of a Roman April kindling into May, was in the atmosphere around them; but when Miriam saw that involuntary movement, and heard that sigh of relief (for so she interpreted it), a shiver ran through her frame, as if the iciest wind of the Apennines were blowing over her.

"He has done himself a greater wrong than I dreamed of," thought she, with unutterable compassion. "Alas! it was a sad mistake! He might have had a kind of bliss in the consequences of this deed, had he been impelled to it by a love vital enough to survive the frenzy of that terrible moment—mighty enough to make its own law, and justify itself against the natural remorse. But to have perpetrated a dreadful murder (and such was his crime, unless love, annihilating moral distinctions, made it otherwise) on no better warrant than a boy's idle fantasy! I pity him from the very depths of my soul! As for myself, I am past my own or other's pity."

She arose from the young man's side, and stood before him with a sad, commiserating aspect; it was the look of a ruined soul, bewailing, in him, a grief less than what her profounder sympathies imposed upon herself.

"Donatello, we must part," she said, with melancholy firmness. "Yes; leave me! Go back to your old tower, which overlooks the green valley you have told me of, among the Apennines. Then, all that has passed will be recognized as but an ugly dream. For, in dreams, the conscience

sleeps, and we often stain ourselves with guilt
of which we should be incapable in our waking
moments. The deed you seemed to do, last night,
was no more than such a dream; there was as
little substance in what you fancied yourself doing.
Go, and forget it all!"

"Ah, that terrible face!" said Donatello,
pressing his hands over his eyes. "Do you call
that unreal?"

"Yes; for you beheld it with dreaming eyes,"
replied Miriam. "It was unreal; and, that you
may feel it so, it is requisite that you see this face
of mine no more. Once, you may have thought
it beautiful; now, it has lost its charm. Yet it
would still retain a miserable potency to bring
back the past illusion, and, in its train, the
remorse and anguish that would darken all your
life. Leave me, therefore, and forget me."

"Forget you, Miriam!" said Donatello, roused
somewhat from his apathy of despair. "If I
could remember you, and behold you, apart from
that frightful visage which stares at me over your

shoulder, that were a consolation, at least, if not
a joy."

"But since that visage haunts you along with
mine," rejoined Miriam, glancing behind her,
"we needs must part. Farewell, then! But
if ever—in distress, peril, shame, poverty, or
whatever anguish is most poignant, whatever
burden heaviest—you should require a life to
be given wholly, only to make your own a little
easier, then summon me! As the case now stands
between us, you have bought me dear, and find
me of little worth. Fling me away, therefore!
May you never need me more! But, if otherwise,
a wish—almost an unuttered wish—will bring me
to you!"

She stood a moment, expecting a reply. But
Donatello's eyes had again fallen on the ground,
and he had not, in his bewildered mind and over-
burdened heart, a word to respond.

"That hour I speak of may never come,"
said Miriam. "So farewell—farewell for ever."

"Farewell," said Donatello.

His voice hardly made its way through the environment of unaccustomed thoughts and emotions which had settled over him like a dense and dark cloud. Not improbably, he beheld Miriam through so dim a medium that she looked visionary; heard her speak only in a thin, faint echo.

She turned from the young man, and, much as her heart yearned towards him, she would not profane that heavy parting by an embrace, or even a pressure of the hand. So soon after the semblance of such mighty love, and after it had been the impulse to so terrible a deed, they parted, in all outward show, as coldly as people part whose whole mutual intercourse has been encircled within a single hour.

And Donatello, when Miriam had departed, stretched himself at full length on the stone bench, and drew his hat over his eyes, as the idle and light-hearted youths of dreamy Italy are accustomed to do, when they lie down in the first convenient shade, and snatch a noon-day-slumber. A stupor was upon him, which he mistook for such drowsiness as he had known in his innocent past life. But, by and by, he raised himself slowly and left the garden. Sometimes poor Donatello started, as if he heard a shriek; sometimes he shrank back, as if a face, fearful to behold, were thrust close to his own. In this dismal mood, bewildered with the novelty of sin and grief, he had little left of that singular resemblance, on account of which, and for their sport, his three friends had fantastically recognized him as the veritable Faun of Praxiteles.

CHAPTER VII.

MIRIAM AND HILDA.

On leaving the Medici Gardens, Miriam felt herself astray in the world; and having no special reason to seek one place more than another, she suffered chance to direct her steps as it would. Thus it happened, that, involving herself in the crookedness of Rome, she saw Hilda's tower rising before her, and was put in mind to climb up to the young girl's eyrie, and ask why she had broken her engagement at the church of the Capuchins. People often do the idlest acts of their lifetime in their heaviest and most anxious moments; so that it would have been no wonder had Miriam been impelled only by so slight a motive of curiosity as we have indicated. But she remembered, too, and with a quaking heart, what the sculptor had mentioned of Hilda's retracing her steps towards the courtyard of the Palazzo Caffarelli in quest of Miriam herself. Had she been compelled to choose between infamy in the eyes of the whole world, or in Hilda's eyes alone, she would unhesitatingly have accepted the former, on condition of remaining spotless in the estimation of her white-souled friend. This possibility, therefore, that Hilda had witnessed the scene of the past night, was unquestionably the cause that drew Miriam to the tower, and made her linger and falter as she approached it.

As she drew near, there were tokens to which her disturbed mind gave a sinister interpretation. Some of her friend's airy family, the doves, with their heads imbedded disconsolately in their bosoms, were huddled in a corner of the piazza; others had alighted on the heads, wings, shoulders, and trumpets of the marble angels which adorned the façade of the neighbouring church; two or three had betaken them-

selves to the Virgin's shrine; and as many as
could find room were sitting on Hilda's win-
dow-sill. But all of them, so Miriam fancied,
had a look of weary expectation and disappointment—no flights, no flutterings, no cooing
murmur; something that ought to have made
their day glad and bright, was evidently left
out of this day's history. And, furthermore,
Hilda's white window-curtain was closely drawn,
with only that one little aperture at the side,
which Miriam remembered noticing the night
before.

"Be quiet," said Miriam to her own heart,
pressing her hand hard upon it. "Why shouldst
thou throb now?—Hast thou not endured more
terrible things than this?"

Whatever were her apprehensions, she would
not turn back. It might be—and the solace
would be worth a world—that Hilda, knowing
nothing of the past night's calamity, would greet
her friend with a sunny smile, and so restore
a portion of the vital warmth, for lack of which

her soul was frozen. But could Miriam, guilty as she was, permit Hilda to kiss her cheek, to clasp her hand, and thus be no longer so unspotted from the world as heretofore.

"I will never permit her sweet touch again," said Miriam, toiling up the staircase, "if I can find strength of heart to forbid it. But, oh! it would be so soothing in this wintry fever-fit of my heart. There can be no harm to my white Hilda in one parting kiss. That shall be all!"

But, on reaching the upper landing-place, Miriam paused, and stirred not again till she had brought herself to an immoveable resolve.

"My lips, my hand, shall never meet Hilda's more," said she.

Meanwhile, Hilda sat listlessly in her painting-room. Had you looked into the little adjoining chamber, you might have seen the slight imprint of her figure on the bed, but would also have detected at once that the white counterpane had not been turned down. The pillow was more disturbed; she had turned her face upon it, the poor child, and bedewed it with some of those tears (among the most chill and forlorn that gush from human sorrow) which the innocent heart pours forth, at its first actual discovery that sin is in the world. The young and pure are not apt to find out that miserable truth until it is brought home to them by the guiltiness of some trusted friend. They may have heard much of the evil of the world, and seem to know it, but only as an impalpable theory. In due time, some mortal, whom they reverence too highly, is commissioned by Providence to teach them this direful lesson; he perpetrates a sin; and Adam falls anew, and Paradise, heretofore in unfaded bloom, is lost again, and closed for ever, with the fiery swords gleaming at its gates.

The chair in which Hilda sat was near the portrait of Beatrice Cenci, which had not yet been taken from the easel. It is a peculiarity of this picture, that its profoundest expression

eludes a straightforward glance, and can only
be caught by side glimpses, or when the eye
falls casually upon it; even as 'if the painted
face had a life and consciousness of its own,
and, resolving not to betray its secret of grief
or guilt, permitted the true tokens to come
forth only when it imagined itself unseen. No
other such magical effect has ever been wrought
by pencil.

Now, opposite the easel hung a looking-glass,
in which Beatrice's face and Hilda's were both
reflected. In one of her weary, nerveless changes
of position, Hilda happened to throw her eyes
on the glass, and took in both these images at
one unpremeditated glance. She fancied—nor
was it without horror—that Beatrice's expression, seen aside and vanishing in a moment,
had been depicted in her own face likewise,
and flitted from it as timorously.

"Am I, too, stained with guilt?" thought the
poor girl, hiding her face in her hands.

Not so, thank Heaven! But, as regards

Beatrice's picture, the incident suggests a theory which may account for its unutterable grief and mysterious shadow of guilt, without detracting from the purity which we love to attribute to that ill-fated girl. Who, indeed, can look at that mouth—with its lips half apart, as innocent as a baby's that has been crying—and not pronounce Beatrice sinless! It was the intimate consciousness of her father's sin that threw its shadow over her, and frightened her into a remote and inaccessible region, where no sympathy could come. It was the knowledge of Miriam's guilt, that lent the same expression to Hilda's face.

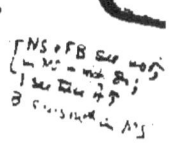

But Hilda nervously moved her chair, so that the images in the glass should be no longer visible. She now watched a speck of sunshine that came through a shuttered window, and crept from object to object, indicating each with a touch of its bright finger, and then letting them all vanish successively. In like manner, her mind, so like sunlight in its natural cheerfulness, went from thought to thought, but found nothing that it could dwell upon for comfort. Never before had this young, energetic, active spirit known what it is to be despondent. It was the unreality of the world that made her so. Her dearest friend, whose heart seemed the most solid and richest of Hilda's possessions, had no existence for her any more; and in that dreary void, out of which Miriam had disappeared, the substance, the truth, the integrity of life, the motives of effort, the joy of success, had departed along with her.

It was long past noon, when a step came up the staircase. It had passed beyond the limits where there was communication with the lower regions of the palace, and was mounting the successive flights which led only to Hilda's precincts. Faint as the tread was, she heard and recognized it. It startled her into sudden life. Her first impulse was to spring to the door of the studio, and fasten it with lock and bolt. But a second thought made her feel that this would be an unworthy cowardice, on her own part, and also that Miriam—only yesterday her closest friend—had a right to be told, face to face, that thenceforth they must be for ever strangers.

She heard Miriam pause, outside of the door. We have already seen what was the latter's resolve with respect to any kiss or pressure of the hand between Hilda and herself. We know not what became of the resolution. As Miriam was of a highly impulsive character, it may have vanished at the first sight of Hilda; but, at all events, she appeared to have dressed herself up in a garb of sunshine, and was disclosed, as the door swung open, in all the glow of her remarkable beauty. The truth was, her heart leaped convulsively towards the only refuge that it had, or hoped. She forgot, just one instant, all cause for holding herself aloof. Ordinarily there was a certain reserve in Miriam's demonstrations of affection, in consonance with the delicacy of her friend. To-day, she opened her arms to take Hilda in.

"Dearest, darling Hilda!" she exclaimed. "It gives me new life to see you!"

Hilda was standing in the middle of the room. When her friend made a step or two from the door, she put forth her hands with an involuntary repellent gesture, so expressive, that Miriam at once felt a great chasm opening itself between them two. They might gaze at one another from the opposite side, but without the possibility of ever meeting more; or, at least, since the chasm could never be bridged over, they must tread the whole round of Eternity to meet on the other side. There was even a terror in the thought of their meeting again. It was as if Hilda or Miriam were dead, and could no longer hold intercourse without violating a spiritual law.

Yet, in the wantonness of her despair, Miriam made one more step towards the friend whom she had lost.

"Do not come nearer, Miriam!" said Hilda.

Her look and tone were those of sorrowful entreaty, and yet they expressed a kind of confidence, as if the girl were conscious of a safeguard that could not be violated.

"What has happened between us, Hilda?" asked Miriam. "Are we not friends?"

"No, no!" said Hilda, shuddering.

"At least, we have been friends," continued Miriam. "I loved you dearly! I love you still! You were to me as a younger sister; yes, dearer than sisters of the same blood; for you and I were so lonely, Hilda, that the whole world pressed us together by its solitude and strangeness. Then, will you not touch my hand? Am I not the same as yesterday?"

"Alas! no, Miriam!" said Hilda.

"Yes, the same—the same for you, Hilda," rejoined her lost friend. "Were you to touch my hand, you would find it as warm to your grasp as ever. If you were sick or suffering, I would watch night and day for you. It is in such simple offices that true affection shows itself; and so I speak of them. Yet now, Hilda, your very look seems to put me beyond the limits of humankind!"

"It is not I, Miriam," said Hilda; "not I that have done this."

"You, and you only, Hilda," replied Miriam, stirred up to make her own cause good, by the repellent force which her friend opposed to her. "I am a woman, as I was yesterday; endowed with the same truth of nature, the same warmth of heart, the same genuine and earnest love, which you have always known in me. In any regard that concerns yourself, I am not changed. And believe me, Hilda, when a human being has chosen a friend out of all the world, it is only some faithlessness between themselves, rendering true intercourse impossible, that can justify either friend in severing the bond. Have I deceived you? Then cast me off! Have I wronged you personally? Then forgive me, if you can. But, have I sinned against God and man, and deeply sinned? Then be more my friend than ever, for I need you more.

"Do not bewilder me thus, Miriam!" exclaimed Hilda, who had not forborne to express, by look and gesture, the anguish which this interview inflicted on her. "If I were one of God's angels, with a nature incapable of stain, and garments that never could be spotted, I would keep ever at your side, and try to lead you upward. But I am a poor, lonely girl, whom God has set here in an evil world, and given her only a white robe, and bid her wear it back to Him, as white as when she put it on. Your powerful magnetism would be too much for me. The pure, white atmosphere, in which I try to discern what things are good and true, would be discoloured. And, therefore, Miriam, before it is too late, I mean to put faith in this awful heart-quake, which warns me henceforth to avoid you."

"Ah, this is hard! Ah, this is terrible!"

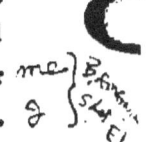

murmured Miriam, dropping her forehead in her hands. In a moment or two she looked up again, as pale as death, but with a composed countenance. "I always said, Hilda, that you were merciless; for I had a perception of it, even while you loved me best. You have no sin, nor any conception of what it is; and therefore you are so terribly severe! As an angel, you are not amiss; but, as a human creature, and a woman among earthly men and women, you need a sin to soften you."

"God forgive me," said Hilda, "if I have said a needlessly cruel word!"

"Let it pass," answered Miriam. "I, whose heart it has smitten upon, forgive you. And tell me, before we part forever, what have you seen or known of me, since we last met?"

"A terrible thing, Miriam," said Hilda, growing paler than before.

"Do you see it written in my face, or painted in my eyes?" inquired Miriam, her trouble seeking relief in a half-frenzied raillery. "I would fain know how it is that Providence, or fate, brings eye-witnesses to watch us, when we fancy ourselves acting in the remotest privacy. Did all Rome see it, then? Or, at least, our merry company of artists? Or is it some blood-stain on me, or death-scent in my garments? They say that monstrous deformities sprout out of fiends, who once were lovely angels. Do you perceive such in me, already? Tell me, by our past friendship, Hilda, all you know."

Thus adjured, and frightened by the wild emotion which Miriam could not suppress, Hilda strove to tell what she had witnessed.

"After the rest of the party had passed on, I went back to speak to you," she said; "for there seemed to be a trouble on your mind, and I wished to share it with you, if you could permit me. The door of the little courtyard was partly shut; but I pushed it open, and saw you within, and Donatello, and a third person,

whom I had before noticed in the shadow of a niche. He approached you, Miriam. You knelt to him. I saw Donatello spring upon him! I would have shrieked, but my throat was dry. I would have rushed forward; but my limbs seemed rooted to the earth.—It was all like a flash of lightning. A look passed from your eyes to Donatello's—a look——"

"Yes, Hilda, yes!" exclaimed Miriam, with intense eagerness. "Do not pause now! That look?"

"It revealed all your heart, Miriam," continued Hilda, covering her eyes as if to shut out the recollection; "a look of hatred, triumph, vengeance, and, as it were, joy at some unhoped-for relief."

"Ah! Donatello was right, then," murmured Miriam, who shook throughout all her frame. "My eyes bade him do it! Go on, Hilda."

"It all passed so quickly—all like a glare of lightning," said Hilda, "and yet it seemed to me that Donatello had paused, while one might draw a breath. But that look!—Ah, Miriam, spare me. Need I tell more?"

"No more; there needs no more, Hilda," replied Miriam, bowing her head, as if listening to a sentence of condemnation from a supreme tribunal. "It is enough! You have satisfied my mind on a point where it was greatly disturbed. Henceforward, I shall be quiet. Thank you, Hilda."

She was on the point of departing, but turned back again from the threshold.

"This is a terrible secret to be kept in a young girl's bosom," she observed; "what will you do with it, my poor child?"

"Heaven help and guide me," answered Hilda, bursting into tears; "for the burden of it crushes me to the earth! It seems a crime to know of such a thing, and to keep it to myself. It knocks within my heart continually, threatening, imploring, insisting to be let out! Oh, my mother! my mother! Were she yet living, I would travel over land and sea to tell her this dark secret, as I told all the little troubles of my infancy. But I am alone—alone! Miriam, you were my dearest, only friend. Advise me what to do."

This was a singular appeal, no doubt, from the stainless maiden to the guilty woman, whom she had just banished from her heart for ever. But it bore striking testimony to the impression which Miriam's natural uprightness and impulsive generosity had made on the friend who knew her best; and it deeply comforted the poor criminal, by proving to her that the bond between Hilda and herself was vital yet.

As far as she was able, Miriam at once responded to the girl's cry for help.

"If I deemed it good for your peace of mind," she said, "to bear testimony against me for this deed, in the face of all the world, no consideration of myself should weigh with me an instant. But I believe that you would find no relief in such a course. What men call justice lies chiefly in outward formalities, and has never the close application and fitness that would be satisfactory to a soul like yours. I cannot be fairly tried and judged before an earthly tribunal; and of this, Hilda, you would perhaps become fatally conscious, when it was too late. Roman justice, above all things, is a byword. What have you to do with it? Leave all such thoughts aside! Yet, Hilda, I would not have you keep my secret imprisoned in your heart, if it tries to leap out, and stings you, like a wild, venomous thing, when you thrust it back again. Have you no other friend, now that you have been forced to give me up?"

"No other," answered Hilda, sadly.

"Yes; Kenyon!" rejoined Miriam.

"He cannot be my friend," said Hilda, "because—because—I have fancied that he sought to be something more."

"Fear nothing!" replied Miriam, shaking her head, with a strange smile. "This story will frighten his new-born love out of its little life, if that be what you wish. Tell him the secret, then, and take his wise and honourable counsel as to what should next be done. I know not what else to say."

"I never dreamed," said Hilda,—" how could you think it?—of betraying you to justice. But I see how it is, Miriam. I must keep your secret, and die of it, unless God sends me some relief by methods which are now beyond my power to imagine. It is very dreadful. Ah! now I understand how the sins of generations past have created an atmosphere of sin for those that follow. While there is a single guilty person in the universe, each innocent one must feel his innocence tortured by that guilt. Your deed, Miriam, has darkened the whole sky!"

Poor Hilda turned from her unhappy friend, and, sinking on her knees in a corner of the chamber, could not be prevailed upon to utter another word. And Miriam, with a long regard from the threshold, bade farewell to this doves' nest, this one little nook of pure thoughts and innocent enthusiasms, into which she had brought such trouble. Every crime destroys more Edens than our own!

CHAPTER VIII.

THE TOWER AMONG THE APENNINES.

It was in June, that the sculptor, Kenyon, arrived on horseback at the gate of an ancient country-house (which, from some of its features, might almost be called a castle) situated in a part of Tuscany somewhat remote from the ordinary track of tourists. Thither we must now accompany him, and endeavour to make our story flow onward, like a streamlet, past a gray tower that rises on the hillside, overlooking a spacious valley, which is set in the grand framework of the Apennines.

The sculptor had left Rome with the retreating tide of foreign residents. For, as summer approaches, the Niobe of Nations is made to bewail anew, and doubtless with sincerity, the

loss of that large part of her population, which
she derives from other lands, and on whom
depends much of whatever remnant of prosperity
she still enjoys. Rome, at this season, is pervaded and overhung with atmospheric terrors,
and insulated within a charmed and deadly circle.
The crowd of wandering tourists betake themselves to Switzerland, to the Rhine, or, from
this central home of the world, to their native
homes in England or America, which they are
apt thenceforward to look upon as provincial,
after once having yielded to the spell of the
Eternal City. The artist, who contemplates an
indefinite succession of winters in this home of
art (though his first thought was merely to
improve himself by a brief visit) goes forth, in
the summer time, to sketch scenery and costume
among the Tuscan hills, and pour, if he can,
the purple air of Italy over his canvas. He
studies the old schools of art in the mountain
towns where they were born, and where they
are still to be seen in the faded frescoes of Giotto

and Cimabue, on the walls of many a church, or
in the dark chapels, in which the sacristan
draws aside the veil from a treasured picture of
Perugino. Thence, the happy painter goes to
walk the long, bright galleries of Florence, or
to steal glowing colours from the miraculous
works, which he finds in a score of Vene-
tian palaces. Such summers as these, spent
amid whatever is exquisite in art, or wild and
picturesque in nature, may not inadequately
repay him for the chill neglect and disappointment through which he has probably languished,
in his Roman winter. This sunny, shadowy,
breezy, wandering life, in which he seeks for
beauty as his treasure, and gathers for his
winter's honey what is but a passing fragrance
to all other men, is worth living for, come afterwards what may. Even if he die unrecognized, the
artist has had his share of enjoyment and success.

Kenyon had seen, at a distance of many miles,
the old villa or castle, towards which his journey
lay, looking from its height over a broad expanse

of valley. As he drew nearer, however, it had been hidden among the inequalities of the hillside, until the winding road brought him almost to the iron gateway. The sculptor found this substantial barrier fastened with lock and bolt. There was no bell, nor other instrument of sound; and, after summoning the invisible garrison with his voice, instead of a trumpet, he had leisure to take a glance at the exterior of the fortress.

About thirty yards within the gateway rose a square tower, lofty enough to be a very prominent object in the landscape, and more than sufficiently massive in proportion to its height. Its antiquity was evidently such, that, in a climate of more abundant moisture, the ivy would have mantled it from head to foot in a garment that might, by this time, have been centuries old, though ever new. In the dry Italian air, however, Nature had only so far adopted this old pile of stonework as to cover almost every hand's-breadth of it with close clinging lichens and yellow moss; and the immemorial growth of these kindly productions rendered the general hue of the tower soft and venerable, and took away the aspect of nakedness which would have made its age drearier than now.

Up and down the height of the tower were scattered three or four windows, the lower ones grated with iron bars, the upper ones vacant both of window-frames and glass. Besides these larger openings, there were several loopholes and little square apertures, which might be supposed to light the staircase, that doubtless climbed the interior towards the battlemented and machicolated summit. With this last-mentioned warlike garniture upon its stern old head and brow, the tower seemed evidently a stronghold of times long past. Many a crossbowman had shot his shafts from those windows and loopholes, and from the vantage height of those gray battlements; many a flight of arrows, too, had hit all round about the embrasures above, or the apertures below, where the helmet of a defender had momentarily glimmered. On festal nights, moreover, a hundred lamps had often gleamed afar over the valley, suspended from the iron hooks that were ranged for the purpose beneath the battlements and every window.

Connected with the tower, and extending behind it, there seemed to be a very spacious residence, chiefly of more modern date. It perhaps owed much of its fresher appearance, however, to a coat of stucco and yellow wash, which is a sort of renovation very much in vogue with the Italians. Kenyon noticed over a doorway, in the portion of the edifice immediately adjacent to the tower, a cross, which, with a bell suspended above the roof, indicated that this was a consecrated precinct, and the chapel of the mansion.

Meanwhile, the hot sun so incommoded the unsheltered traveller, that he shouted forth another impatient summons. Happening, at the same moment, to look upward, he saw a figure leaning from an embrasure of the battlements, and gazing down at him.

"Ho, Signor Count!" cried the sculptor, waving his straw hat, for he recognized the face, after a moment's doubt. "This is a warm reception, truly! Pray bid your porter let me in, before the sun shrivels me quite into a cinder."

"I will come myself," responded Donatello, flinging down his voice out of the clouds, as it were. "old Thomaso and old Stella are both asleep, no doubt, and the rest of the people are in the vineyard. But I have expected you, and you are welcome!"

The young count—as perhaps we had better designate him in his ancestral tower—vanished from the battlements; and Kenyon saw his figure appear successively at each of the windows, as he descended. On every reappearance, he turned his face towards the sculptor and gave a nod and smile; for a kindly impulse prompted him thus to assure his visitor of a welcome, after keeping him so long at an inhospitable threshold.

Kenyon, however (naturally and professionally expert at reading the expression of the human countenance), had a vague sense that this was not the young friend whom he had known so familiarly in Rome; not the sylvan and untutored youth, whom Miriam, Hilda, and himself, had liked, laughed at, and sported with; not the Donatello whose identity they had so playfully mixed up with that of the Faun of Praxiteles.

Finally, when his host had emerged from a side-portal of the mansion, and approached the gateway, the traveller still felt that there was something lost, or something gained (he hardly knew which), that set the Donatello of to-day irreconcileably at odds with him of yesterday. His very gait showed it, in a certain gravity, a weight and measure of step, that had nothing in common with the irregular buoyancy which used to distinguish him. His face was paler and thinner, and the lips less full, and less apart.

"I have looked for you a long while," said Donatello; and, though his voice sounded differently, and cut out its words more sharply than had been its wont, still there was a smile shining on his face, that, for the moment, quite brought back the Faun. "I shall be more cheerful, perhaps, now that you have come. It is very solitary here."

"I have come slowly along, often lingering, often turning aside," replied Kenyon; "for I found a great deal to interest me in the mediæval sculpture hidden away in the churches hereabouts. An artist, whether painter or sculptor, may be pardoned for loitering through such a region. But what a fine old tower! Its tall front is like a page of black-letter, taken from the history of the Italian republics."

"I know little or nothing of its history," said the count, glancing upward at the battlements, where he had just been standing. "But I

thank my forefathers for building it so high. I
like the windy summit better than the world
below, and spend much of my time there, now-
a-days."

"It is a pity you are not a star-gazer,"
observed Kenyon, also looking up. "It is higher
than Galileo's tower, which I saw, a week or
two ago, outside of the walls of Florence."

"A star-gazer? I am one," replied Donatello.
"I sleep in the tower, and often watch very
late on the battlements. There is a dismal old
staircase to climb, however, before reaching the
top, and a succession of dismal chambers, from
story to story. Some of them were prison chambers in times past, as old Tomaso will tell you."

The repugnance intimated in his tone, at the
idea of this gloomy staircase and these ghostly,
dimly lighted rooms, reminded Kenyon of the
original Donatello, much more than his present
custom of midnight vigils on the battlements.

"I shall be glad to share your watch," said
the guest; "especially by moonlight. The pro-

spect of this broad valley must be very fine. But I was not aware, my friend, that these were your country habits. I have fancied you in a sort of Arcadian life, tasting rich figs, and squeezing the juice out of the sunniest grapes, and sleeping soundly, all night, after a day of simple pleasures."

"I may have known such a life, when I was younger," answered the count, gravely. "I am not a boy now. Time flies over us, but leaves its shadow behind."

The sculptor could not but smile at the triteness of the remark, which, nevertheless had a kind of originality as coming from Donatello. He had thought it out from his own experience, and perhaps considered himself as communicating a new truth to mankind.

They were now advancing up the courtyard; and the long extent of the villa, with its iron-barred lower windows and balconied upper ones, became visible, stretching back towards a grove of trees.

"At some period of your family history," observed Kenyon, "the Counts of Monte Beni must have led a patriarchal life in this vast house. A great-grandsire and all his descendants might find ample verge here, and with space, too, for each separate brood of little ones to play within its own precincts. Is your present household a large one?"

"Only myself," answered Donatello, "and Tomaso, who has been butler since my grandfather's time, and old Stella, who goes sweeping and dusting about the chambers, and Girolamo, the cook, who has but an idle life of it. He shall send you up a chicken forthwith. But, first of all, I must summon one of the contadini from the farmhouse yonder, to take your horse to the stable."

Accordingly, the young count shouted amain, and with such effect, that, after several repetitions of the outcry, an old gray woman protruded her head and a broom-handle from a chamber-window; the venerable butler emerged from a recess in the side of the house, where was a well, or reservoir, in which he had been cleansing a small wine-cask; and a sun-burnt contadino, in his shirt-sleeves, showed himself on the outskirts of the vineyard, with some kind of a farming tool in his hand. Donatello found employment for all these retainers in providing accommodation for his guest and steed, and then ushered the sculptor into the vestibule of the house.

It was a square and lofty entrance room, which, by the solidity of its construction, might have been an Etruscan tomb, being paved and walled with heavy blocks of stone, and vaulted almost as massively overhead. On two sides, there were doors, opening into long suites of ante-rooms and saloons; on the third side, a stone staircase, of spacious breadth, ascending, by dignified degrees and with wide resting-places, to another floor of similar extent. Through one of the doors, which was ajar, Kenyon beheld an almost interminable vista of apartments, opening one beyond the other, and reminding him of the hundred rooms in Blue Beard's castle, or the countless halls in some palace of the Arabian Nights.

It must have been a numerous family, indeed, that could ever have sufficed to people with human life so large an abode as this, and impart social warmth to such a wide world within doors. The sculptor confessed to himself, that Donatello could allege reason enough for growing melancholy, having only his own personality to vivify it all.

"How a woman's face would brighten it up!" he ejaculated, not intending to be overheard.

But, glancing at Donatello, he saw a stern and sorrowful look in his eyes, which altered his youthful face as much as if it had seen thirty years of trouble; and, at the same moment, old Stella showed herself through one of the doorways, as the only representative of her sex at Monte Beni.

CHAPTER IX.

SUNSHINE.

"Come," said the count, "I see you already find the old house dismal. So do I, indeed! And yet it was a cheerful place in my boyhood. But, you see, in my father's days (and the same was true of all my endless line of grandfathers, as I have heard), there used to be uncles, aunts, and all manner of kindred, dwelling together as one family. They were a merry and kindly race of people, for the most part, and kept one another's hearts warm."

"Two hearts might be enough for warmth," observed the sculptor, "even in so large a house as this. One solitary heart, it is true, may be apt to shiver a little. But, I trust, my friend, that the genial blood of your race still flows in many veins besides your own?"

"I am the last," said Donatello, gloomily. "They have all vanished from me, since my childhood. Old Tomaso will tell you that the air of Monte Beni is not so favourable to length of days as it used to be. But that is not the secret of the quick extinction of my kindred."

"Then you are aware of a more satisfactory reason?" suggested Kenyon.

"I thought of one, the other night, while I was gazing at the stars," answered Donatello; "but, pardon me, I do not mean to tell it. One cause, however, of the longer and healthier life of my forefathers, was, that they had many pleasant customs, and means of making themselves glad, and their guests and friends along with them. Now-a-days we have but one!"

"And what is that?" asked the sculptor.

"You shall see!" said his young host.

By this time, he had ushered the sculptor into one of the numberless saloons; and, calling for refreshment, old Stella placed a cold fowl upon the table, and quickly followed it with a savoury omelette, which Girolamo had lost no time in preparing. She also brought some cherries, plums, and apricots, and a plate full of particularly delicate figs, of last year's growth. The butler showing his white head at the door, his master beckoned to him.

"Tomaso, bring some Sunshine!" said he.

The readiest method of obeying this order, one might suppose, would have been, to fling wide the green window-blinds, and let the glow of the summer noon into the carefully shaded room. But, at Monte Beni, with provident caution against the wintry days, when there is little sunshine, and the rainy ones, when there is none, it was the hereditary custom to keep their Sunshine stored away in the cellar. Old Tomaso quickly produced some of it in a small, straw-covered flask, out of which he extracted the cork, and inserted a little cotton wool, to absorb the olive oil that kept the precious liquid from the air.

"This is a wine," observed the count, "the secret of making which has been kept in our family for centuries upon centuries; nor would it avail any man to steal the secret, unless he could also steal the vineyard, in which alone the Monte Beni grape can be produced. There is little else left me, save that patch of vines. Taste some of their juice, and tell me whether it is worthy to be called Sunshine! for that is its name."

"A glorious name, too!" cried the sculptor.

"Taste it," said Donatello, filling his friend's glass and pouring likewise a little into his own. "But first smell its fragrance; for the wine is very lavish of it, and will scatter it all abroad."

"Ah, how exquisite!" said Kenyon. "No other wine has a bouquet like this. The flavour must be rare indeed, if it fulfil the promise of this fragrance, which is like the airy sweetness of youthful hopes, that no realities will ever satisfy!"

This invaluable liquor was of a pale golden

hue, like other of the rarest Italian wines, and, if carelessly and irreligiously quaffed, might have been mistaken for a very fine sort of Champagne. It was not, however, an effervescing wine, although its delicate piquancy produced a somewhat similar effect upon the palate. Sipping, the guest longed to sip again; but the wine demanded so deliberate a pause, in order to detect the hidden peculiarities and subtle exquisiteness of its flavour, that to drink it was really more a moral than a physical enjoyment. There was a deliciousness in it that eluded analysis, and—like whatever else is superlatively good—was perhaps better appreciated in the memory than by present consciousness. One of its most ethereal charms lay in the transitory life of the wine's richest qualities; for, while it required a certain leisure and delay, yet, if you lingered too long upon the draught, it became disenchanted both of its fragrance and its flavour.

The lustre should not be forgotten, among

the other admirable endowments of the Monte
Beni wine; for, as it stood in Kenyon's glass, a
little circle of light glowed on the table round
about it, as if it were really so much golden
sunshine.

"I feel myself a better man for that ethereal
potation," observed the sculptor. "The finest
Orvieto, or that famous wine, the Est Est Est
of Montefiascone, is vulgar in comparison. This
is surely the wine of the Golden Age, such as
Bacchus himself first taught mankind to press
from the choicest of his grapes. My dear count,
why is it not illustrious? The pale, liquid gold,
in every such flask as that, might be solidified
into golden scudi, and would quickly make you
a millionaire!"

Tomaso, the old butler, who was standing by
the table, and enjoying the praises of the wine
quite as much as if bestowed upon himself,
made answer,—

"We have a tradition, signore," said he, "that
this rare wine of our vineyard would lose all

its wonderful qualities, if any of it were sent to market. The Counts of Monte Beni have never parted with a single flask of it for gold. At their banquets, in the olden time, they have entertained princes, cardinals, and once an emperor, and once a pope, with this delicious wine, and always, even to this day, it has been their custom to let it flow freely, when those whom they love and honour sit at the board. But the grand duke himself could not drink that wine, except it were under this very roof!"

"What you tell me, my good friend," replied Kenyon, "makes me venerate the Sunshine of Monte Beni even more abundantly than before. As I understand you, it is a sort of consecrated juice, and symbolizes the holy virtues of hospitality and social kindness?"

"Why, partly so, signore," said the old butler, with a shrewd twinkle in his eye; "but, to speak out all the truth, there is another excellent reason why neither a cask nor a flask of our precious vintage should ever be sent to

/market. The wine, signore, is so fond of its native home, that a transportation of even a few miles, turns it quite sour. And yet it is a wine that keeps well in the cellar, underneath this floor, and gathers fragrance, flavour, and brightness, in its dark dungeon. That very flask of Sunshine, now, has kept itself for you, sir guest, (as a maid reserves her sweetness till her lover comes for it) ever since a merry vintage-time, when the Signor Count here was a boy!"

"You must not wait for Tomaso to end his discourse about the wine, before drinking off your glass," observed Donatello. "When once the flask is uncorked, its finest qualities lose little time in making their escape. I doubt whether your last sip will be quite so delicious as you found the first."

And, in truth, the sculptor fancied that the Sunshine became almost imperceptibly clouded, as he approached the bottom of the flask. The effect of the wine, however, was a gentle exhilaration, which did not so speedily pass away.

Being thus refreshed, Kenyon looked around him at the antique saloon in which they sat. It was constructed in a most ponderous style, with a stone floor, on which heavy pilasters were planted against the wall, supporting arches that crossed one another in the vaulted ceiling. The upright walls, as well as the compartments of the roof, were completely covered with frescoes, which doubtless had been brilliant when first executed, and perhaps for generations afterwards. The designs were of a festive and joyous character, representing Arcadian scenes, where nymphs, fauns, and satyrs, disported themselves among mortal youths and maidens; and Pan, and the god of wine, and he of sunshine and music, disdained not to brighten some sylvan merry-making with the scarcely veiled glory of their presence. A wreath of dancing figures, in admirable variety of shape and motion, was festooned quite round the cornice of the room.

In its first splendour, the saloon must have presented an aspect both gorgeous and enlivening; for it invested some of the cheerfullest ideas and emotions of which the human mind is susceptible with the external reality of beautiful form, and rich, harmonious glow and variety of colour. But the frescoes were now very ancient. They had been rubbed and scrubbed by old Stella and many a predecessor, and had been defaced in one spot, and retouched in another, and had peeled from the wall in patches, and had hidden some of their brightest portions under dreary dust, till the joyousness had quite vanished out of them all. It was often difficult to puzzle out the design; and even where it was more readily intelligible, the figures showed like the ghosts of dead and buried joys—the closer their resemblance to the happy past, the gloomier now. For it is thus, that with only an inconsiderable change, the gladdest objects and existences become the saddest; hope fading into disappointment; joy darkening into grief, and festal splendour into funereal duskiness; and all evolving, as their moral, a grim identity between gay things and sorrowful ones. Only give them a little time, and they turn out to be just alike!

"There has been much festivity in this saloon, if I may judge by the character of its frescoes," remarked Kenyon, whose spirits were still upheld by the mild potency of the Monte Beni wine. "Your forefathers, my dear count, must have been joyous fellows, keeping up the vintage merriment throughout the year. It does me good to think of them gladdening the hearts of men and women, with their wine of Sunshine, even in the Iron age, as Pan and Bacchus, whom we see yonder, did in the Golden one!"

"Yes, there have been merry times in the banquet-hall of Monte Beni, even within my own remembrance," replied Donatello, looking gravely at the painted walls. "It was meant for mirth, as you see; and when I brought my own cheerfulness into the saloon, these frescoes looked cheerful too. But methinks they have all faded since I saw them last."

"It would be a good idea," said the sculptor, falling into his companion's vein, and helping him out with an illustration which Donatello himself could not have put into shape, "to convert this saloon into a chapel; and when the priest tells his hearers of the instability of earthly joys, and would show how drearily they vanish, he may point to these pictures, that were so joyous, and are so dismal. He could not illustrate his theme so aptly in any other way."

"True, indeed," answered the count, his former simplicity strangely mixing itself up with an experience that had changed him; "and yonder, where the minstrels used to stand, the altar shall be placed. A sinful man might do all the more effective penance in this old banquet-hall."

"But I should regret to have suggested so ungenial a transformation in your hospitable saloon," continued Kenyon, duly noting the change in Donatello's characteristics. "You

startle me, my friend, by so ascetic a design!
It would hardly have entered your head, when
we first met. Pray do not—if I may take the
freedom of a somewhat elder man to advise
you," added he, smiling—"pray do not, under a
notion of improvement, take upon yourself to
be sombre, thoughtful, and penitential, like all
the rest of us."

Donatello made no answer, but sat awhile,
appearing to follow with his eyes one of the
figures, which was repeated many times over in
the groups upon the walls and ceiling. It formed
the principal link of an allegory, by which (as
is often the case in such pictorial designs) the
whole series of frescoes were bound together,
but which it would be impossible, or, at least,
very wearisome, to unravel. The sculptor's eyes
took a similar direction, and soon began to trace
through the vicissitudes—once gay, now sombre
—in which the old artist had involved it, the
same individual figure. He fancied a resemblance in it to Donatello himself; and it put

him in mind of one of the purposes with which he had come to Monte Beni.

"My dear count," said he, "I have a proposal to make. You must let me employ a little of my leisure in modelling your bust. You remember what a striking resemblance we all of us—Hilda, Miriam, and I—found between your features and those of the Faun of Praxiteles. Then, it seemed an identity; but now that I know your face better, the likeness is far less apparent. Your head in marble would be a treasure to me. Shall I have it?"

"I have a weakness which I fear I cannot overcome," replied the count, turning away his face. "It troubles me to be looked at steadfastly."

"I have observed it since we have been sitting here, though never before," rejoined the sculptor. "It is a kind of nervousness, I apprehend, which you caught in the Roman air, and which grows upon you, in your solitary life. It need be no hindrance to my taking your bust; for

I will catch the likeness and expression by side-glimpses, which (if portrait painters and bust-makers did but know it) always bring home richer results than a broad stare."

"You may take me if you have the power," said Donatello; but, even as he spoke, he turned away his face; "and if you can see what makes me shrink from you, you are welcome to put it in the bust. It is not my will, but my necessity, to avoid men's eyes. Only," he added, with a smile which made Kenyon doubt whether he might not as well copy the Faun as model a new bust, "only, you know, you must not insist on my uncovering these ears of mine!"

"Nay; I never should dream of such a thing," answered the sculptor, laughing as the young count shook his clustering curls. "I could not hope to persuade you, remembering how Miriam once failed!"

Nothing is more unaccountable than the spell that often lurks in a spoken word. A thought

may be present to the mind, so distinctly that
no utterance could make it more so; and two
minds may be conscious of the same thought,
in which one or both take the profoundest interest;
but as long as it remains unspoken, their
familiar talk flows quietly over the hidden idea,
as a rivulet may sparkle and dimple over something
sunken in its bed. But, speak the word;
and it is like bringing up a drowned body out
of the deepest pool of the rivulet, which has
been aware of the horrible secret all along, in
spite of its smiling surface.

And even so, when Kenyon chanced to make
a distinct reference to Donatello's relations with
Miriam (though the subject was already in both
their minds), a ghastly emotion rose up out of
the depths of the young count's heart. He
trembled either with anger or terror, and glared
at the sculptor with wild eyes, like a wolf that
meets you in the forest, and hesitates whether to
flee or turn to bay. But, as Kenyon still looked
calmly at him, his aspect gradually became less

disturbed, though far from resuming its former quietude.

"You have spoken her name," said he, at last, in an altered and tremulous tone; "tell me, now, all that you know of her."

"I scarcely think that I have any later intelligence than yourself," answered Kenyon; "Miriam left Rome at about the time of your own departure. Within a day or two after our last meeting at the church of the Capuchins, I called at her studio and found it vacant. Whither she has gone, I cannot tell."

Donatello asked no further questions.

They rose from table, and strolled together about the premises, whiling away the afternoon with brief intervals of unsatisfactory conversation, and many shadowy silences. The sculptor had a perception of change in his companion— possibly of growth and development, but certainly of change—which saddened him, because it took away much of the simple grace that was the best of Donatello's peculiarities.

Kenyon betook himself to repose that night in a grim, old, vaulted apartment, which, in the lapse of five or six centuries, had probably been the birth, bridal, and death chamber of a great many generations of the Monte Beni family. He was aroused, soon after daylight, by the clamour of a tribe of beggars, who had taken their stand in a little rustic lane, that crept beside that portion of the villa, and were addressing their petitions to the open windows. By and by, they appeared to have received alms, and took their departure.

"Some charitable Christian has sent those vagabonds away," thought the sculptor, as he resumed his interrupted nap; "who could it be? Donatello has his own rooms in the tower; Stella, Tomaso, and the cook are a world's width off; and I fancied myself the only inhabitant in this part of the house."

In the breadth and space which so delightfully characterize an Italian villa, a dozen guests might have had each his suite of apartments without infringing upon one another's precincts. But, so far as Kenyon knew, he was the only visitor beneath Donatello's widely extended roof.

CHAPTER X.

THE PEDIGREE OF MONTE BENI.

From the old butler, whom he found to be a very gracious and affable personage, Kenyon soon learned many curious particulars about the family history and hereditary peculiarities of the Counts of Monte Beni. There was a pedigree, the later portion of which—that is to say, for a little more than a thousand years—a genealogist would have found delight in tracing out, link by link, and authenticating by records and documentary evidences. It would have been as difficult, however, to follow up the stream of Donatello's ancestry to its dim source, as travellers have found it to reach the mysterious fountains of the Nile. And, far beyond the region of definite and demonstrable fact, a romancer might have strayed into a region of old poetry, where the rich soil, so long uncultivated and untrodden, had lapsed into nearly its primeval state of wilderness. Among those antique paths, now overgrown with tangled and riotous vegetation, the wanderer must needs follow his own guidance, and probably arrive nowhither at last.

The race of Monte Beni, beyond a doubt, was one of the oldest in Italy, where families appear to survive at least, if not to flourish, on their half-decayed roots, oftener than in England or France. It came down in a broad track from the Middle Ages; but, at epochs anterior to those, it was distinctly visible in the gloom of the period before chivalry put forth its flower; and further still, we are almost afraid to say, it was seen, though with a fainter and wavering course, in the early morn of Christendom, when the Roman Empire had hardly begun to show symptoms of decline. At that venerable distance, the heralds gave up the lineage in despair.

But where written record left the genealogy

of Monte Beni, tradition took it up, and carried
it without dread or shame beyond the Imperial
ages into the times of the Roman republic;
beyond those, again, into the epoch of kingly
rule. Nor even so remotely among the mossy
centuries did it pause, but strayed onward into
that gray antiquity of which there is no token
left, save its cavernous tombs, and a few bronzes,
and some quaintly wrought ornaments of gold,
and gems with mystic figures and inscriptions.
There, or thereabouts, the line was supposed to
have had its origin in the sylvan life of Etruria,
while Italy was yet guiltless of Rome.

Of course, as we regret to say, the earlier and
very much the larger portion of this respectable
descent—and the same is true of many briefer
pedigrees—must be looked upon as altogether
mythical. Still, it threw a romantic interest
around the unquestionable antiquity of the Monte
Beni family, and over that tract of their own
vines and fig-trees, beneath the shade of which
they had unquestionably dwelt for immemorial

ages. And there they had laid the foundations of their tower, so long ago that one-half of its height was said to be sunken under the surface, and to hide subterranean chambers which once were cheerful with the olden sunshine.

One story, or myth, that had mixed itself up with their mouldy genealogy, interested the sculptor by its wild, and perhaps grotesque, yet not unfascinating peculiarity. He caught at it the more eagerly, as it afforded a shadowy and whimsical semblance of explanation for the likeness which he, with Miriam and Hilda, had seen, or fancied, between Donatello and the Faun of Praxiteles.

The Monte Beni family, as this legend averred, drew their origin from the Pelasgic race, who peopled Italy in times that may be called prehistoric. It was the same noble breed of men, of Asiatic birth, that settled in Greece; the same happy and poetic kindred who dwelt in Arcadia, and—whether they ever lived such life or not—enriched the world with dreams, at least, and fables, lovely, if unsubstantial, of a Golden Age. In those delicious times, when deities and demigods appeared familiarly on earth, mingling with its inhabitants as friend with friend—when nymphs, satyrs, and the whole train of classic faith or fable, hardly took pains to hide themselves in the primeval woods—at that auspicious period, the lineage of Monte Beni had its rise. Its progenitor was a being not altogether human, yet partaking so largely of the gentlest human qualities, as to be neither awful nor shocking to the imagination. A sylvan creature, native among the woods, had loved a mortal maiden, and—perhaps by kindness, and the subtle courtesies which love might teach to his simplicity, or possibly by a ruder wooing—had won her to his haunts. In due time, he gained her womanly affection; and, making their bridal bower, for aught we know, in the hollow of a great tree, the pair spent a happy wedded life in that ancient neighborhood, where now stood Donatello's tower.

From this union sprang a vigorous progeny that took its place unquestioned among human families. In that age, however, and long afterwards, it showed the ineffaceable lineaments of its wild paternity; it was a pleasant and kindly race of men, but capable of savage fierceness, and never quite restrainable within the trammels of social law. They were strong, active, genial, cheerful as the sunshine, passionate as the tornado. Their lives were rendered blissful by an unsought harmony with nature.

But, as centuries passed away, the Faun's wild blood had necessarily been attempered with constant intermixtures from the more ordinary streams of human life. It lost many of its original qualities, and served, for the most part, only to bestow an unconquerable vigour, which kept the family from extinction, and enabled them to make their own part good throughout the perils and rude emergencies of their interminable descent. In the constant wars with which Italy was plagued, by the dissensions of her petty states and republics, there was a demand for native hardihood.

The successive members of the Monte Beni family showed valour and policy enough, at all events, to keep their hereditary possessions out of the clutch of grasping neighbours, and probably differed very little from the other feudal barons with whom they fought and feasted. Such a degree of conformity with the manners of the generations, through which it survived, must have been essential to the prolonged continuance of the race.

It is well known, however, that any hereditary peculiarity—as a supernumerary finger, or an anomalous shape of feature, like the Austrian lip—is wont to show itself in a family after a very wayward fashion. It skips at its own pleasure along the line, and, latent for half a century or so, crops out again in a great-grandson. And thus, it was said, from a period beyond human memory or record, there had ever and anon been a descendant of the Monte Benis bearing nearly all the characteristics that were attributed to the original founder of the race. Some traditions even went so far as to enumerate the ears, covered with a delicate fur, and shaped like a pointed leaf, among the proofs of authentic descent which were seen in these favoured individuals. We appreciate the beauty of such tokens of a nearer kindred to the great family of nature than other mortals bear; but it would be idle to ask credit for a statement which might be deemed to partake so largely of the grotesque.

But it was indisputable that, once in a century, or oftener, a son of Monte Beni gathered into himself the scattered qualities of his race, and reproduced the character that had been assigned to it from immemorial times. Beautiful, strong, brave, kindly, sincere, of honest impulses, and endowed with simple tastes and the love of homely pleasures, he was believed to possess gifts by which he could associate himself with the wild things of the forests, and with the fowls of the air, and could feel a sympathy even with the trees, among which it was his joy to dwell. On the other hand, there were deficiencies both of intellect and heart, and especially, as it seemed, in the development of the higher portion of man's nature. These defects were less perceptible in early youth, but showed themselves more strongly with advancing age, when, as the animal spirits settled down upon a lower level, the representative of the Monte Benis was apt to become sensual, addicted to gross pleasures, heavy, unsympathizing, and insulated within the narrow limits of a surly selfishness.

A similar change, indeed, is no more than what we constantly observe to take place in persons who are not careful to substitute other graces for those which they inevitably lose along with the quick sensibility and joyous vivacity of youth. At worst, the reigning Count of Monte Beni, as his hair grew white, was still a jolly old fellow over his flask of wine—the wine that Bacchus himself was fabled to have taught his

sylvan ancestor how to express, and from what
choicest grapes, which would ripen only in a
certain divinely favoured portion of the Monte
Beni vineyard.

The family, be it observed, were both proud
and ashamed of these legends; but whatever part
of them they might consent to incorporate into
their ancestral history, they steadily repudiated
all that referred to their one distinctive feature,
the pointed and furry ears. In a great many
years past, no sober credence had been yielded
to the mythical portion of the pedigree. It
might, however, be considered as typifying some
such assemblage of qualities—in this case, chiefly
remarkable for their simplicity and naturalness
—as, when they reappear in successive generations, constitute what we call family character.
The sculptor found, moreover, on the evidence
of some old portraits, that the physical features
of the race had long been similar to what he
now saw them in Donatello. With accumu-
lating years, it is true, the Monte Beni face

had a tendency to look grim and savage; and, in two or three instances, the family pictures glared at the spectator in the eyes, like some surly animal, that had lost its good-humour when it outlived its playfulness.

The young count accorded his guest full liberty to investigate the personal annals of these pictured worthies, as well as all the rest of his progenitors; and ample materials were at hand in many chests of worm-eaten papers and yellow parchments, that had been gathering into larger and dustier piles ever since the dark ages. But, to confess the truth, the information afforded by these musty documents was so much more prosaic than what Kenyon acquired from Tomaso's legends, that even the superior authenticity of the former could not reconcile him to its dulness.

What especially delighted the sculptor, was the analogy between Donatello's character, as he himself knew it, and those peculiar traits which the old butler's narrative assumed to have been long hereditary in the race. He was amused at finding, too, that not only Tomaso, but the peasantry of the estate and neighbouring village recognized his friend as a genuine Monte Beni, of the original type. They seemed to cherish a great affection for the young count, and were full of stories about his sportive childhood; how he had played among the little rustics, and been at once the wildest and the sweetest of them all; and how, in his very infancy, he had plunged into the deep pools of the streamlets, and never been drowned, and had clambered to the topmost branches of tall trees without ever breaking his neck. No such mischance could happen to the sylvan child, because, handling all the elements of nature so fearlessly and freely, nothing had either the power or the will to do him harm.

He grew up, said these humble friends, the playmate not only of all mortal kind, but of creatures of the woods; although, when Kenyon pressed them for some particulars of this latter mode of companionship, they could remember little more than a few anecdotes of a pet fox, which used to growl and snap at everybody save Donatello himself.

But they enlarged—and never were weary of the theme—upon the blithesome effects of Donatello's presence in his rosy childhood and budding youth. Their hovels had always glowed like sunshine when he entered them; so that, as the peasants expressed it, their young master had never darkened a doorway in his life. He was the soul of vintage festivals. While he was a mere infant, scarcely able to run alone, it had been the custom to make him tread the wine-press with his tender little feet, if it were only to crush one cluster of the grapes. And the grape-juice that gushed beneath his childish tread, be it ever so small in quantity, sufficed to impart a pleasant flavour to a whole cask of wine. The race of Monte Beni—so these rustic chroniclers assured the sculptor—had possessed the gift from the oldest of old times of expressing good wine from ordinary grapes, and a ravishing liquor from the choice growth of their vineyard.

In a word, as he listened to such tales as these, Kenyon could have imagined that the valleys and hill-sides about him were a veritable Arcadia, and that Donatello was not merely a sylvan faun, but the genial wine-god in his very person. Making many allowances for the poetic fancies of Italian peasants, he set it down for fact, that his friend, in a simple way, and among rustic folks, had been an exceedingly delightful fellow in his younger days.

But the contadini sometimes added, shaking their heads and sighing, that the young count was sadly changed, since he went to Rome. The village girls now missed the merry smile with which he used to greet them.

The sculptor inquired of his good friend Tomaso, whether he, too, had noticed the shadow which was said to have recently fallen over Donatello's life.

B Emerson.
Sat 51

"Ah, yes, signor!" answered the old butler, "it is even so, since he came back from that wicked and miserable city. The world has grown either too evil, or else too wise and sad, for such men as the old Counts of Monte Beni used to be. His very first taste of it, as you see, has changed and spoilt my poor young lord. There had not been a single count in the family these hundred years and more, who was so true a Monte Beni, of the antique stamp, as this poor signorino; and now, it brings the tears into my eyes to hear him sighing over a cup of Sunshine! Ah, it is a sad world now!"

"Then, you think there was a merrier world once?" asked Kenyon.

"Surely, signor," said Tomaso; "a merrier world, and merrier Counts of Monte Beni to live in it! Such tales of them as I have heard, when I was a child on my grandfather's knee! The good old man remembered a lord of Monte Beni—at least, he had heard of such a one, though I will not make oath upon the holy crucifix that my grandsire lived in his time— who used to go into the woods and call pretty damsels out of the fountains, and out of the trunks of the old trees. That merry lord was known to dance with them a whole long summer afternoon! When shall we see such frolics in our days?"

"Not soon, I am afraid," acquiesced the sculptor. "You are right, excellent Tomaso: the world is sadder now!"

And, in truth, while our friend smiled at these wild fables, he sighed in the same breath, to think how the once genial earth produces, in every successive generation, fewer flowers than used to gladden the preceding ones. Not that the modes and seeming possibilities of human enjoyment are rarer in our refined and softened era—on the contrary, they never before were nearly so abundant—but that mankind are getting so far beyond the childhood of their race that they scorn to be happy any longer. A

simple and joyous character can find no place
for itself among the sage and sombre figures
that would put his unsophisticated cheerfulness
to shame. The entire system of man's affairs,
as at present established, is built up purposely
to exclude the careless and happy soul. The
very children would upbraid the wretched individual who should endeavour to take life and
the world as what we might naturally suppose
them meant for—a place and opportunity for
enjoyment.

It is the iron rule in our day to require an
object and a purpose in life. It makes us all
parts of a complicated scheme of progress, which
can only result in our arrival at a colder and
drearier region than we were born in. It insists
upon everybody's adding somewhat—a mite, perhaps, but earned by incessant effort—to an accumulated pile of usefulness, of which the only
use will be, to burden our posterity with even
heavier thoughts and more inordinate labour than
our own. No life now wanders like an un-

fettered stream; there is a mill-wheel for the tiniest rivulet to turn. We go all wrong, by too strenuous a resolution to go all right.

Therefore it was so, at least, the sculptor thought, although partly suspicious of Donatello's darker misfortune—that the young count found it impossible now-a-days to be what his forefathers had been. He could not live their healthy life of animal spirits, in their sympathy with nature, and brotherhood with all that breathed around them. Nature, in beast, fowl, and tree, and earth, flood, and sky, is what it was of old; but sin, care, and self-consciousness have set the human portion of the world askew; and thus the simplest character is ever the soonest to go astray.

"At any rate, Tomaso," said Kenyon, doing his best to comfort the old man, "let us hope that your young lord will still enjoy himself at vintage-time. By the aspect of the vineyard, I judge that this will be a famous year for the golden wine of Monte Beni. As long as your grapes produce that admirable liquor, sad as you think the world, neither the count nor his guests will quite forget to smile."

"Ah, signor," rejoined the butler with a sigh, "but he scarcely wets his lips with the sunny juice."

"There is yet another hope," observed Kenyon; "the young count may fall in love, and bring home a fair and laughing wife to chase the gloom out of yonder old, frescoed saloon. Do you think he could do a better thing, my good Tomaso?"

"Maybe not, signor," said the sage butler, looking earnestly at him; "and, maybe, not a worse!"

The sculptor fancied that the good old man had it partly in his mind to make some remark, or communicate some fact, which, on second thoughts, he resolved to keep concealed in his own breast. He now took his departure cellarward, shaking his white head and muttering to himself, and did not reappear till dinner-time, when he favoured Kenyon, whom he had taken far into his good graces, with a choicer flask of Sunshine than had yet blessed his palate.

To say the truth, this golden wine was no unnecessary ingredient towards making the life of Monte Beni palatable. It seemed a pity that Donatello did not drink a little more of it, and go jollily to bed at least, even if he should awake with an accession of darker melancholy the next morning.

Nevertheless, there was no lack of outward means for leading an agreeable life in the old villa. Wandering musicians haunted the precincts of Monte Beni, where they seemed to claim a prescriptive right; they made the lawn and shrubbery tuneful with the sound of fiddle, harp, and flute, and now and then with the tangled squeaking of a bagpipe. Improvvisatori likewise came and told tales or recited verses to the contadini—among whom Kenyon often was an auditor—after their day's work in the vineyard. Jugglers, too, obtained permission to do feats of magic in the hall, where they set even the sage Tomaso, and Stella, Girolamo, and the peasant girls from the farmhouse, all of a broad grin, between merriment and wonder. These good people got food and lodging for their pleasant pains, and some of the small wine of Tuscany, and a reasonable handful of the Grand Duke's copper coin, to keep up the hospitable renown of Monte Beni. But very seldom had they the young count as a listener, or a spectator.

There were sometimes dances by moonlight on the lawn; but never, since he came from Rome, did Donatello's presence deepen the blushes of the pretty contadinas, or his footstep weary out the most agile partner or competitor, as once it was sure to do.

Paupers—for this kind of vermin infested the house of Monte Beni worse than any other spot in beggar-haunted Italy—stood beneath all the windows, making loud supplication, or even establishing themselves on the marble steps of the grand entrance. They ate and drank, and filled their bags, and pocketed the little money that was given them, and went forth on their devious ways, showering blessings innumerable on the mansion and its lord, and on the souls of his deceased forefathers, who had always been just such simpletons as to be compassionate to beggary. But, in spite of their favourable prayers, by which Italian philanthropists set great store, a cloud seemed to hang over these once Arcadian precincts, and to be darkest around the summit of the tower where Donatello was wont to sit and brood.

CHAPTER XL

MYTHS.

AFTER the sculptor's arrival, however, the young count sometimes came down from his forlorn elevation, and rambled with him among the neighboring woods and hills. He led his friend to many enchanting nooks, with which he himself had been familiar in his childhood. But of late, as he remarked to Kenyon, a sort of strangeness had overgrown them, like clusters of dark shrubbery, so that he hardly recognized the places which he had known and loved so well.

To the sculptor's eye, nevertheless, they were still rich with beauty. They were picturesque in that sweetly impressive way, where wildness, in a long lapse of years, has crept over scenes that have been once adorned with the careful art and toil of man; and when man could do no more for them, time and nature came, and wrought hand in hand to bring them to a soft and venerable perfection. There grew the fig-tree that had run wild, and taken to wife the vine, which likewise had gone rampant out of all human control; so that the two wild things had tangled and knotted themselves into a wild marriage-bond, and hung their various progeny —the luscious figs, the grapes, oozy with the southern juice, and both endowed with a wild flavour that added the final charm—on the same bough together.

In Kenyon's opinion, never was any other nook so lovely as a certain little dell which he and Donatello visited. It was hollowed in among the hills, and open to a glimpse of the broad, fertile valley. A fountain had its birth here, and fell into a marble basin, which was all covered with moss and shaggy with water-weeds. Over the gush of the small stream, with an urn in her arms, stood a marble nymph, whose nakedness the moss had kindly clothed as with a garment; and the long trails and tresses of the maiden-hair had done what they could in the poor thing's behalf, by hanging themselves about her waist. In former days—it might be a remote antiquity—this lady of the fountain had first received the infant tide into her urn and poured it thence into the marble basin. But now the sculptured urn had a great crack, from top to bottom; and the discontented nymph was compelled to see the basin fill itself through a channel which she could not control, although with water long ago consecrated to her.

For this reason, or some other, she looked terribly forlorn; and you might have fancied that the whole fountain was but the overflow of her lonely tears.

"This was a place that I used greatly to delight in," remarked Donatello, sighing. "As a child, and as a boy, I have been very happy here."

"And, as a man, I should ask no fitter place to be happy in," answered Kenyon. "But you, my friend, are of such a social nature, that I should hardly have thought these lonely haunts would take your fancy. It is a place for a poet to dream in, and people it with the beings of his imagination."

"I am no poet, that I know of," said Donatello, "but yet, as I tell you, I have been very happy here, in the company of this fountain and this nymph. It is said that a Faun, my oldest forefather, brought home hither to this very spot a human maiden, whom he loved and wedded. This spring of delicious water was their household well."

"It is a most enchanting fable!" exclaimed Kenyon; "that is, if it be not a fact."

"And why not a fact?" said the simple Donatello. "There is likewise another sweet old story connected with this spot. But, now that I remember it, it seems to me more sad than sweet, though formerly the sorrow, in

which it closes, did not so much impress me.
If I had the gift of tale-telling, this one would
be sure to interest you mightily."

"Pray tell it," said Kenyon; "no matter
whether well or ill. These wild legends have
often the most powerful charm when least art-
fully told."

So the young count narrated a myth of one
of his progenitors, he might have lived a century ago, or a thousand years, or before the
Christian epoch, for anything that Donatello
knew to the contrary, who had made acquaintance with a fair creature belonging to this
fountain. Whether woman or sprite was a mystery, as was all else about her, except that her
life and soul were somehow interfused throughout the gushing water. She was a fresh, cool,
dewy thing, sunny and shadowy, full of pleasant
little mischiefs, fitful and changeable with the
whim of the moment, but yet as constant as
her native stream, which kept the same gush
and flow for ever, while marble crumbled over

and around it. The fountain woman loved the
youth— a knight, as Donatello called him—for,
according to the legend, his race was akin to
hers. At least, whether kin or no, there had
been friendship and sympathy of old betwixt
an ancestor of his, with furry ears, and the
long-lived lady of the fountain. And, after all
those ages, she was still as young as a May-
morning, and as frolicksome as a bird upon a
tree, or a breeze that makes merry with the
leaves.

She taught him how to call her from her
pebbly source, and they spent many a happy
hour together, more especially in the fervour of
the summer days. For often as he sat waiting
for her by the margin of the spring, she would
suddenly fall down around him in a shower of
sunny rain-drops, with a rainbow glancing
through them, and forthwith gather herself up
into the likeness of a beautiful girl, laughing—
or was it the warble of the rill over the pebbles?
—to see the youth's amazement.

Thus, kind maiden that she was, the hot atmosphere became deliciously cool and fragrant for this favoured knight; and, furthermore, when he knelt down to drink out of the spring, nothing was more common than for a pair of rosy lips to come up out of its little depths, and touch his mouth with the thrill of a sweet, cool, dewy kiss!

"It is a delightful story for the hot noon of your Tuscan summer," observed the sculptor, at this point. "But the deportment of the watery lady must have had a most chilling influence in mid-winter. Her lover would find it, very literally, a cold reception!"

"I suppose," said Donatello, rather sulkily, "you are making fun of the story. But I see nothing laughable in the thing itself, nor in what you say about it."

He went on to relate, that for a long while, the knight found infinite pleasure and comfort in the friendship of the fountain nymph. In his merriest hours, she gladdened him with her sportive humour. If ever he was annoyed with earthly trouble, she laid her moist hand upon his brow, and charmed the fret and fever quite away.

But one day—one fatal noontide—the young knight came rushing with hasty and irregular steps to the accustomed fountain. He called the nymph; but—no doubt because there was something unusual and frightful in his tone—she did not appear, nor answer him. He flung himself down, and washed his hands and bathed his feverish brow in the cool, pure water. And then, there was a sound of woe; it might have been a woman's voice; it might have been only the sighing of the brook over the pebbles. The water shrank away from the youth's hands, and left his brow as dry and feverish as before.

Donatello here came to a dead pause.

"Why did the water shrink from this unhappy knight?" inquired the sculptor.

"Because he had tried to wash off a blood-

stain!" said the young count, in a horror-
stricken whisper. "The guilty man had polluted
the pure water. The nymph might have comforted him in sorrow, but could not cleanse his
conscience of a crime."

"And did he never behold her more?" asked
Kenyon.

"Never but once," replied his friend. "He
never beheld her blessed face but once again;
and then there was a blood-stain on the poor
nymph's brow; it was the stain his guilt had
left in the fountain where he tried to wash it
off. He mourned for her his whole life long,
and employed the best sculptor of the time to
carve this statue of the nymph from his description of her aspect. But, though my ancestor would fain have had the image wear her
happiest look, the artist, unlike yourself, was so
impressed with the mournfulness of the story,
that, in spite of his best efforts, he made her
forlorn, and for ever weeping, as you see!"

Kenyon found a certain charm in this simple

legend. Whether so intended or not, he understood it as an apologue, typifying the soothing and genial effects of an habitual intercourse with nature, in all ordinary cares and griefs; while, on the other hand, her mild influences fall short in their effect upon the ruder passions, and are altogether powerless in the dread fever-fit or deadly chill of guilt.

"Do you say," he asked, "that the nymph's face has never since been shown to any mortal? Methinks, you, by your native qualities, are as well entitled to her favour as ever your progenitor could have been. Why have you not summoned her?"

"I called her often when I was a silly child," answered Donatello; and he added, in an inward voice,—"Thank Heaven, she did not come!"

"Then you never saw her?" said the sculptor.

"Never in my life!" rejoined the count. "No, my dear friend, I have not seen the nymph; although here, by her fountain, I used to make many strange acquaintances; for, from my earliest childhood, I was familiar with whatever creatures haunt the woods. You would have laughed to see the friends I had among them; yes, among the wild, nimble things, that reckon man their deadliest enemy! How it was first taught me, I cannot tell; but there was a charm—a voice, a murmur, a kind of chaunt—by which I called the woodland inhabitants, the furry people, and the feathered people, in a language that they seemed to understand."

"I have heard of such a gift," responded the sculptor gravely, "but never before met with a person endowed with it. Pray, try the charm; and lest I should frighten your friends away, I will withdraw into this thicket, and merely peep at them."

"I doubt," said Donatello, "whether they will remember my voice now. It changes, you know, as the boy grows towards manhood."

Nevertheless, as the young count's good-nature and easy persuasibility were among his best characteristics, he set about complying with Kenyon's request. The latter, in his concealment among the shrubberies, heard him send forth a sort of modulated breath, wild, rude, yet harmonious. It struck the auditor as at once the strangest and the most natural utterance that had ever reached his ears. Any idle boy, it should seem, singing to himself, and setting his wordless song to no other or more definite tune than the play of his own pulses, might produce a sound almost identical with this; and yet, it was as individual as a murmur of the breeze. Donatello tried it, over and over again, with many breaks, at first, and pauses of uncertainty; then with more confidence, and a fuller swell, like a wayfarer groping out of obscurity into the light, and moving with freer footsteps as it brightens around him.

Anon, his voice appeared to fill the air, yet not with an obtrusive clangour. The sound was of a murmurous character, soft, attractive, persuasive, friendly. The sculptor fancied that such might have been the original voice and utterance of the natural man, before the sophistication of the human intellect formed what we now call language. In this broad dialect—broad as the sympathies of nature—the human brother might have spoken to his inarticulate brotherhood that prowl the woods, or soar upon the wing, and have been intelligible, to such extent as to win their confidence.

The sound had its pathos too. At some of its simple cadences, the tears came quietly into Kenyon's eyes. They welled up slowly from his heart, which was thrilling with an emotion more delightful than he had often felt before, but which he forbore to analyze, lest, if he seized it, it should at once perish in his grasp.

Donatello paused two or three times, and seemed to listen; then recommencing, he poured his spirit and life more earnestly into the strain. And, finally—or else the sculptor's hope and imagination deceived him — soft treads were audible upon the fallen leaves. There was a rustling among the shrubbery; a whirr of wings, moreover, that hovered in the air. It may have been all an illusion; but Kenyon fancied that he could distinguish the stealthy, cat-like movement of some small forest citizen, and that he could even see its doubtful shadow, if not really its substance. But, all at once, whatever might be the reason, there ensued a hurried rush and scamper of little feet; and then the sculptor heard a wild, sorrowful cry, and through the crevices of the thicket beheld Donatello fling himself on the ground.

Emerging from his hiding-place, he saw no living thing, save a brown lizard (it was of the tarantula species) rustling away through the sunshine. To all present appearance, this venomous reptile was the only creature that had responded to the young count's efforts to renew his intercourse with the lower orders of nature.

"What has happened to you?" exclaimed Kenyon, stooping down over his friend, and wondering at the anguish which he betrayed.

"Death, death!" sobbed Donatello. "They know it!"

He grovelled beside the fountain, in a fit of such passionate sobbing and weeping, that it seemed as if his heart had broken, and spilt its wild sorrows upon the ground. His unrestrained grief and childish tears made Kenyon sensible in how small a degree the customs and restraints of society had really acted upon this young man, in spite of the quietude of his ordinary deportment. In response to his friend's efforts to console him, he murmured words hardly more articulate than the strange chaunt which he had so recently been breathing into the air.

"They know it!" was all that Kenyon could yet distinguish. "They know it!"

"Who knows it?" asked the sculptor. "And what is it they know?"

"They know it!" repeated Donatello, trembling. "They shun me! All nature shrinks from me, and shudders at me! I live in the midst of a curse, that hems me round with a circle of fire! No innocent thing can come near me."

"Be comforted, my dear friend," said Kenyon, kneeling beside him. "You labour under some illusion, but no curse. As for this strange, natural spell, which you have been exercising, and of which I have heard before, though I never believed in, nor expected to witness it, I am satisfied that you still possess it. It was my own half-concealed presence, no doubt, and some involuntary little movement of mine, that scared away your forest friends."

"They are friends of mine no longer," answered Donatello.

"We all of us, as we grow older," rejoined Kenyon, "lose somewhat of our proximity to nature. It is the price we pay for experience."

"A heavy price, then!" said Donatello, rising from the ground. "But we will speak no more of it. Forget this scene, my dear friend. In your eyes, it must look very absurd. It is a grief, I presume, to all men, to find the pleasant privileges and properties of early life departing from them. That grief has now befallen me. Well; I shall waste no more tears for such a cause!"

Nothing else made Kenyon so sensible of a change in Donatello, as his newly acquired power of dealing with his own emotions, and, after a struggle more or less fierce, thrusting them down into the prison-cells where he usually kept them confined. The restraint which he now put upon himself, and the mask of dull composure which he succeeded in clasping over his still beautiful and once faun-like face, affected the sensitive sculptor more sadly than even the unrestrained passion of the preceding scene. It is a very miserable epoch, when the evil necessities of life, in our tortuous world, first get the better of us so far, as to compel us to attempt throwing a cloud over our transparency. Simplicity increases in value, the longer we can keep it, and the farther we carry it onward into life; the loss of a child's simplicity, in the inevitable lapse of years, causes but a natural sigh or two, because even his mother feared that he could not keep it always. But after a young man has brought it through his childhood, and has still worn it in his bosom, not as an early dew-drop, but as a diamond of pure, white lustre,— it is a pity to lose it, then. And thus, when Kenyon saw how much his friend had now to hide, and how well he hid it, he could have wept, although his tears would have been even idler than those which Donatello had just shed.

They parted on the lawn before the house, the count to climb his tower, and the sculptor to read an antique edition of Dante, which he had found among some old volumes of Catholic devotion, in a seldom-visited room. Tomaso met him in the entrance hall, and showed a desire to speak.

"Our poor signorino looks very sad to-day!" he said.

"Even so, good Tomaso," replied the sculptor. "Would that we could raise his spirits a little!"

"There might be means, signor," answered

the old butler, "if one might but be sure that they were the right ones. We men are but rough nurses for a sick body or a sick spirit."

"Women, you would say, my good friend, are better," said the sculptor, struck by an intelligence in the butler's face. "That is possible! But it depends."

"Ah; we will wait a little longer," said Tomaso, with the customary shake of his head.

CHAPTER XII.

THE OWL TOWER.

"Will you not show me your tower?" said the sculptor one day to his friend.

"It is plainly enough to be seen, methinks," answered the count, with a kind of sulkiness that often appeared in him, as one of the little symptoms of inward trouble.

"Yes; its exterior is visible far and wide," said Kenyon. "But such a gray, moss-grown tower as this, however valuable as an object of scenery, will certainly be quite as interesting inside as out. It cannot be less than six hundred years old; the foundations and lower story are much older than that, I should judge; and traditions probably cling to the walls within quite as plentifully as the gray and yellow lichens cluster on its face without."

"No doubt," replied Donatello, "but I know little of such things, and never could comprehend the interest which some of you Forestieri take in them. A year or two ago an English signor with a venerable white beard—they say he was a magician, too—came hither from as far off as Florence, just to see my tower."

"Ah, I have seen him at Florence," observed Kenyon. "He is a necromancer, as you say, and dwells in an old mansion of the Knights Templars, close by the Ponte Vecchio, with a great many ghostly books, pictures, and antiquities, to make the house gloomy, and one bright-eyed little girl to keep it cheerful!"

"I know him only by his white beard," said Donatello; "but he could have told you a great deal about the tower, and the sieges which it has stood, and the prisoners who have been confined in it. And he gathered up all the traditions of the Monte Beni family, and, among the rest, the sad one which I told you at the fountain, the other day. He had known mighty poets, he said,

in his earlier life; and the most illustrious of them would have rejoiced to preserve such a legend in immortal rhyme—especially if he could have had some of our wine of Sunshine to help out his inspiration!"

"Any man might be a poet, as well as Byron, with such wine and such a theme," rejoined the sculptor. "But, shall we climb your tower? The thunder-storm gathering yonder among the hills will be a spectacle worth witnessing."

"Come, then," said the count, adding, with a sigh, "it has a weary staircase, and dismal chambers, and it is very lonesome at the summit!"

"Like a man's life, when he has climbed to eminence," remarked the sculptor, "or, let us rather say, with its difficult steps, and the dark prison cells you speak of, your tower resembles the spiritual experience of many a sinful soul, which, nevertheless, may struggle upward into the pure air and light of heaven at last!"

Donatello sighed again, and led the way up into the tower.

Mounting the broad staircase that ascended from the entrance hall, they traversed the great wilderness of a house, through some obscure passages, and came to a low, ancient doorway. It admitted them to a narrow turret-stair which zigzagged upward, lighted in its progress by loopholes and iron-barred windows. Reaching the top of the first flight, the count threw open a door of worm-eaten oak, and disclosed a chamber that occupied the whole area of the tower. It was most pitiably forlorn of aspect, with a brick-paved floor, bare holes through the massive walls, grated with iron, instead of windows, and for furniture an old stool, which increased the dreariness of the place tenfold, by suggesting an idea of its having once been tenanted.

"This was a prisoner's cell in the old days," said Donatello; "the white-bearded necromancer, of whom I told you, found out that a certain famous monk was confined here, about five hun-

dred years ago. He was a very holy man, and
was afterwards burned at the stake in the Grand-
ducal Square at Firenze. There have always
been stories, Tomaso says, of a hooded monk
creeping up and down these stairs, or standing
in the doorway of this chamber. It must needs
be the ghost of the ancient prisoner. Do you
believe in ghosts?"

"I can hardly tell," replied Kenyon; "on the
whole, I think not."

"Neither do I," responded the count; "for,
if spirits ever come back, I should surely have
met one within these two months past. Ghosts
never rise! So much I know, and am glad to
know it!"

Following the narrow staircase still higher,
they came to another room of similar size and
equally forlorn, but inhabited by two personages
of a race which from time immemorial have held
proprietorship and occupancy in ruined towers.
These were a pair of owls, who, being doubtless
acquainted with Donatello, showed little sign of

alarm at the entrance of visitors. They gave a dismal croak or two, and hopped aside into the darkest corner; since it was not yet their hour to flap duskily abroad.

"They do not desert me, like my other feathered acquaintances," observed the young count, with a sad smile, alluding to the scene which Kenyon had witnessed at the fountain-side. "When I was a wild, playful boy, the owls did not love me half so well."

He made no further pause here, but led his friend up another flight of steps; while, at every stage, the windows and narrow loopholes afforded Kenyon more extensive eye-shots over hill and valley, and allowed him to taste the cool purity of the mid atmosphere. At length they reached the topmost chamber, directly beneath the roof of the tower.

"This is my own abode," said Donatello; "my own owl's nest."

In fact, the room was fitted up as a bed-chamber, though in a style of the utmost simplicity. It likewise served as an oratory; there being a crucifix in one corner, and a multitude of holy emblems, such as Catholics judge it necessary to help their devotion withal. Several ugly little prints, representing the sufferings of the Saviour, and the martyrdoms of saints, hung on the wall; and, behind the crucifix, there was a good copy of Titian's Magdalen of the Pitti Palace, clad only in the flow of her golden ringlets. She had a confident look (but it was Titian's fault, not the penitent woman's), as if expecting to win heaven by the free display of her earthly charms. Inside of a glass case appeared an image of the sacred Bambino, in the guise of a little waxen boy, very prettily made, reclining among flowers, like a Cupid, and holding up a heart that resembled a bit of red sealing-wax. A small vase of precious marble was full of holy water.

Beneath the crucifix, on a table, lay a human skull, which looked as if it might have been dug up out of some old grave. But, examining it more closely, Kenyon saw that it was carved in gray alabaster, most skilfully done to the death, with accurate imitation of the teeth, the sutures, the empty eye-caverns, and the fragile little bones of the nose. This hideous emblem rested on a cushion of white marble, so nicely wrought that you seemed to see the impression of the heavy skull in a silken and downy substance.

Donatello dipped his fingers into the holy-water vase, and crossed himself. After doing so, he trembled.

"I have no right to make the sacred symbol on a sinful breast!" he said.

"On what mortal breast can it be made then?" asked the sculptor. "Is there one that hides no sin?"

"But these blessed emblems make you smile, I fear," resumed the count, looking askance at his friend. "You heretics, I know, attempt to pray without even a crucifix to kneel at."

"I, at least, whom you call a heretic, re-

verence that holy symbol," answered Kenyon.
"What I am most inclined to murmur at, is
this death's head. I could laugh, moreover, in
its ugly face! It is absurdly monstrous, my
dear friend, thus to fling the dead weight of
our mortality upon our immortal hopes. While
we live on earth, 'tis true we must needs carry
our skeletons about with us; but, for Heaven's
sake, do not let us burden our spirits with them,
in our feeble efforts to soar upward! Believe
me, it will change the whole aspect of death, if
you can once disconnect it, in your idea, with
that corruption from which it disengages our
higher part."

"I do not well understand you," said Donna-
tello; and he took up the alabaster skull, shuddering, and evidently feeling it a kind of penance
to touch it. "I only know that this skull has
been in my family for centuries. Old Tomaso
has a story that it was copied by a famous
sculptor from the skull of that same unhappy
knight who loved the fountain-lady, and lost

her by a blood-stain. He lived and died with a deep sense of sin upon him, and, on his death-bed, he ordained that this token of him should go down to his posterity. And my forefathers, being a cheerful race of men in their natural disposition, found it needful to have the skull often before their eyes, because they dearly loved life and its enjoyments, and hated the very thought of death."

"I am afraid," said Kenyon, "they liked it none the better, for seeing its face under this abominable mask."

Without further discussion, the count led the way up one more flight of stairs, at the end of which they emerged upon the summit of the tower. The sculptor felt as if his being were suddenly magnified a hundredfold; so wide was the Umbrian valley that suddenly opened before him, set in its grand framework of nearer and more distant hills. It seemed as if all Italy lay under his eyes in that one picture. For there was the broad, sunny smile of God, which we fancy to be spread over that favoured land more abundantly than on other regions, and, beneath it, glowed a most rich and varied fertility. The trim vineyards were there, and the fig-trees, and the mulberries, and the smoky-hued tracts of the olive-orchards; there, too, were fields of every kind of grain, among which waved the Indian corn, putting Kenyon in mind of the fondly remembered acres of his father's homestead. White villas, gray convents, church-spires, villages, towns, each with its battlemented walls and towered gateway, were scattered upon this spacious map; a river gleamed across it; and lakes opened their blue eyes in its face, reflecting heaven, lest mortals should forget that better land, when they beheld the earth so beautiful.

What made the valley look still wider, was the two or three varieties of weather that were visible on its surface, all at the same instant of time. Here lay the quiet sunshine; there fell the great black patches of ominous shadow from the clouds; and behind them, like a giant of league-long strides, came hurrying the thunder-storm, which had already swopt midway across the plain. In the rear of the approaching tempest, brightened forth again the sunny splendour, which its progress had darkened with so terrible a frown.

All round this majestic landscape, the bald-peaked or forest-crowned mountains descended boldly upon the plain. On many of their spurs and midway declivities, and even on their summits, stood cities, some of them famous of old; for these had been the seats and nurseries of early Art, where the flower of Beauty sprang out of a rocky soil, and in a high, keen atmosphere, when the richest and most sheltered gardens failed to nourish it.

"Thank God for letting me again behold this scene!" said the sculptor, a devout man in his way, reverently taking off his hat. "I have viewed it from many points, and never without as full a sensation of gratitude as my heart seems capable of feeling. How it strengthens the poor human spirit in its reliance on His providence, to ascend but this little way above the common level, and so attain a somewhat wider glimpse of His dealings with mankind! He doeth all things right! His will be done!"

"You discern something that is hidden from me," observed Donatello, gloomily, yet striving with unwonted grasp to catch the analogies which so cheered his friend. "I see sunshine on one spot, and cloud in another, and no reason for it in either case. The sun on you; the cloud on me! What comfort can I draw from this?"

"Nay; I cannot preach," said Kenyon, "with a page of heaven and a page of earth spread wide open before us! Only begin to read it, and you will find it interpreting itself without the aid of words. It is a great mistake to try to put our best thoughts into human language. When we ascend into the higher regions of emotion and spiritual enjoyment, they are only expressible by such grand hieroglyphics as these around us."

They stood awhile, contemplating the scene; but, as inevitably happens after a spiritual flight, it was not long before the sculptor felt his wings flagging in the rarity of the upper atmosphere. He was glad to let himself quietly downward out of the mid-sky, as it were, and alight on the solid platform of the battlemented tower. He looked about him, and beheld growing out of the stone pavement, which formed the roof, a little shrub, with green and glossy leaves. It was the only green thing there; and heaven knows how its seeds had ever been planted, at that airy height, or how it had found nourishment for its small life, in the chinks of the stones; for it had no earth, and nothing more like soil than the crumbling mortar, which had been crammed into the crevices in a long-past age.

Yet the plant seemed fond of its native site; and Donatello said it had always grown there, from his earliest remembrance, and never, he believed, any smaller or any larger than they saw it now.

"I wonder if the shrub teaches you any good lesson," said he, observing the interest with which Kenyon examined it. "If the wide valley has a great meaning, the plant ought to have at least a little one; and it has been growing on our tower long enough to have learned how to speak it."

"Oh, certainly!" answered the sculptor; "the shrub has its moral, or it would have perished long ago. And, no doubt, it is for your use and edification, since you have had it before your eyes all your lifetime, and now are moved to ask what may be its lesson."

"It teaches me nothing," said the simple Donatello, stooping over the plant, and perplexing himself with a minute scrutiny. "But here was a worm that would have killed it; an ugly creature, which I will fling over the battlements."

CHAPTER XIII.

ON THE BATTLEMENTS.

The sculptor now looked through an embrasure, and threw down a bit of lime, watching its fall, till it struck upon a stone bench at the rocky foundation of the tower, and flew into many fragments.

"Pray pardon me for helping Time to crumble away your ancestral walls," said he. "But I am one of those persons who have a natural tendency to climb heights, and to stand on the verge of them, measuring the depth below. If I were to do just as I like, at this moment, I should fling myself down after that bit of lime. It is a very singular temptation, and all but irresistible; partly, I believe, because it might be so easily done, and partly because such momentous consequences would ensue, without my being compelled to wait a moment for them. Have you never felt this strange impulse of an evil spirit at your back, shoving you towards a precipice?"

"Ah, no!" cried Donatello, shrinking from the battlemented wall with a face of horror. "I cling to life in a way which you cannot conceive; it has been so rich, so warm, so sunny!— and beyond its verge, nothing but the chilly dark! And then a fall from a precipice is such an awful death!"

"Nay; if it be a great height," said Kenyon, "a man would leave his life in the air, and never feel the hard shock at the bottom."

"That is not the way with this kind of death!" exclaimed Donatello, in a low, horror-stricken voice, which grew higher and more full of emotion as he proceeded. "Imagine a fellow-creature—breathing, now, and looking you in the face —and now tumbling down, down, down, with a long shriek wavering after him, all the way!

He does not leave his life in the air! No; but
it keeps in him till he thumps against the stones,
a horribly long while; then, he lies there frightfully quiet, a dead heap of bruised flesh and
broken bones! A quiver runs through the
crushed mass; and no more movement after that!
No; not if you would give your soul to make
him stir a finger! Ah, terrible! Yes, yes; I
would fain fling myself down, for the very dread
of it, that I might endure it once for all, and
dream of it no more!"

"How forcibly—how frightfully you conceive
this!" said the sculptor, aghast at the passionate
horror which was betrayed in the count's words,
and still more in his wild gestures and ghastly
look. "Nay, if the height of your tower affects
your imagination thus, you do wrong to trust
yourself here in solitude, and in the night-time,
and at all unguarded hours. You are not safe
in your chamber. It is but a step or two; and
what if a vivid dream should lead you up hither
at midnight, and act itself out as a reality!"

Donatello had hidden his face in his hands, and was leaning against the parapet.

"No fear of that!" said he. "Whatever the dream may be, I am too genuine a coward to act out my own death in it."

The paroxysm passed away, and the two friends continued their desultory talk, very much as if no such interruption had occurred. Nevertheless, it affected the sculptor with infinite pity to see this young man, who had been born to gladness as an assured heritage, now involved in a misty bewilderment of grievous thoughts, amid which he seemed to go staggering blindfold. Kenyon, not without an unshaped suspicion of the definite fact, knew that his condition must have resulted from the weight and gloom of life, now first, through the agency of a secret trouble, making themselves felt on a character that had heretofore breathed only an atmosphere of joy. The effect of this hard lesson upon Donatello's intellect and disposition was very striking. It was perceptible that he had already had glimpses of strange and subtile matters in those dark caverns, into which all men must descend, if they would know anything beneath the surface and illusive pleasures of existence. And when they emerge, though dazzled and blinded by the first glare of daylight, they take truer and sadder views of life for ever afterwards.

From some mysterious source, as the sculptor felt assured, a soul had been inspired into the young count's simplicity, since their intercourse in Rome. He now showed a far deeper sense, and an intelligence that began to deal with high subjects, though in a feeble and childish way. He evinced, too, a more definite and nobler individuality, but developed out of grief and pain, and fearfully conscious of the pangs that had given it birth. Every human life, if it ascends to truth or delves down to reality, must undergo a similar change; but sometimes, perhaps, the instruction comes without the sorrow; and oftener the sorrow teaches no lesson that abides with us. In Donatello's case, it was pitiful, and almost ludicrous, to observe the confused struggle that he made; how completely he was taken by surprise; how ill-prepared he stood, on this old battle-field of the world, to fight with such an inevitable foe as mortal calamity, and sin for its stronger ally.

"And yet," thought Kenyon, "the poor fellow bears himself like a hero, too! If he would only tell me his trouble, or give me an opening to speak frankly about it, I might help him; but he finds it too horrible to be uttered, and fancies himself the only mortal that ever felt the anguish of remorse. Yes; he believes that nobody ever endured his agony before; so that—sharp enough in itself—it has all the additional zest of a torture just invented to plague him individually."

The sculptor endeavoured to dismiss the painful subject from his mind; and, leaning against the battlements, he turned his face southward and westward, and gazed across the breadth of the valley. His thoughts flow far beyond even those wide boundaries, taking an air-line from Donatello's tower to another turret that ascended into the sky of the summer afternoon, invisibly to him, above the roofs of distant Rome. Then rose tumultuously into his consciousness that strong love for Hilda, which it was his habit to confine in one of the heart's inner chambers, because he had found no encouragement to bring it forward. But now, he felt a strange pull at his heart-strings. It could not have been more perceptible, if all the way between these battlements and Hilda's dovecote had stretched an exquisitely sensitive cord, which, at the hither end, was knotted with his aforesaid heart-strings, and, at the remoter one, was grasped by a gentle hand. His breath grew tremulous. He put his hand to his breast; so distinctly did he seem to feel that cord drawn once and again, and again, as if—though still it was bashfully intimated—there were an importunate demand for his presence. Oh! for the white wings of

Hilda's doves, that he might have flown thither, and alighted at the Virgin's shrine!

But lovers, and Kenyon knew it well, project so lifelike a copy of their mistresses out of their own imaginations, that it can pull at the heart-strings almost as perceptibly as the genuine original. No airy intimations are to be trusted; no evidences of responsive affection less positive than whispered and broken words, or tender pressures of the hand, allowed and half returned, or glances, that distil many passionate avowals into one gleam of richly coloured light. Even these should be weighed rigorously, at the instant; for, in another instant, the imagination seizes on them as its property, and stamps them with its own arbitrary value. But Hilda's maidenly reserve had given her lover no such tokens, to be interpreted either by his hopes or fears.

"Yonder, over mountain and valley, lies Rome," said the sculptor; "shall you return thither in the autumn?"

"Never! I hate Rome," answered Donatello; "and have good cause."

"And yet it was a pleasant winter that we spent there," observed Kenyon, "and with pleasant friends about us. You would meet them again there—all of them."

"All?" asked Donatello.

"All, to the best of my belief," said the sculptor; "but you need not go to Rome to seek them. If there were one of those friends whose life-line was twisted with your own, I am enough of a fatalist to feel assured that you will meet that one again, wander whither you may. Neither can we escape the companions whom Providence assigns for us, by climbing an old tower like this."

"Yet the stairs are steep and dark," rejoined the count; "none but yourself would seek me here, or find me, if they sought."

As Donatello did not take advantage of this opening which his friend had kindly afforded him, to pour out his hidden troubles, the latter again threw aside the subject, and returned to the enjoyment of the scene before him. The thunder-storm, which he had beheld striding across the valley, had passed to the left of Monte Beni, and was continuing its march towards the hills that formed the boundary on the eastward. Above the whole valley, indeed, the sky was heavy with tumbling vapours, interspersed with which were tracts of blue, vividly brightened by the sun; but, in the east, where the tempest was yet trailing its ragged skirts, lay a dusky region of cloud and sullen mist, in which some of the hills appeared of a dark purple hue. Others became so indistinct, that the spectator could not tell rocky height from impalpable cloud. Far into this misty cloud-region, however—within the domain of chaos, as it were—hill-tops were seen brightening in the sunshine; they looked like fragments of the world, broken adrift and based on nothingness, or like portions of a sphere destined to exist, but not yet finally compacted.

The sculptor, habitually drawing many of the images and illustrations of his thoughts from the plastic art, fancied that the scene represented the process of the Creator, when He held the new, imperfect earth in His hand, and modelled it.

"What a magic is in mist and vapour among the mountains!" he exclaimed. "With their help, one single scene becomes a thousand. The cloud-scenery gives such variety to a hilly landscape that it would be worth while to journalize its aspect from hour to hour. A cloud, however, as I have myself experienced, is apt to grow solid and as heavy as a stone the instant that you take in hand to describe it. But, in my own art, I have found great use in clouds. Such silvery ones as those to the northward, for example, have often suggested sculpturesque groups, figures, and attitudes; they are especially rich in attitudes of living repose, which a sculptor only hits upon by the rarest good fortune. When I go back to my dear native land, the clouds along the horizon will be my only gallery of art!"

"I can see cloud-shapes too," said Donatello; "yonder is one that shifts strangely; it has been like people whom I knew. And now, if I watch it a little longer, it will take the figure of a monk reclining, with his cowl about his head and drawn partly over his face, and—well! did I not tell you so?"

"I think," remarked Kenyon, "we can hardly be gazing at the same cloud. What I behold is a reclining figure, to be sure, but feminine, and with a despondent air, wonderfully well expressed in the wavering outline from head to foot. It moves my very heart by something indefinable that it suggests."

"I see the figure, and almost the face," said the count, adding, in a lower voice, "It is Miriam's!"

"No, not Miriam's," answered the sculptor.

While the two gazers thus found their own reminiscences and presentiments floating among the clouds, the day drew to its close, and now showed them the fair spectacle of an Italian sunset. The sky was soft and bright, but not so gorgeous as Kenyon had seen it, a thousand times, in America; for there the western sky is wont to be set aflame with breadths and depths of colour, with which poets seek in vain to dye their verses, and which painters never dare to copy. As beheld from the tower of Monte Beni, the scene was tenderly magnificent, with mild gradations of hue, and a lavish outpouring of gold, but rather such gold as we see on the leaf of a bright flower than the burnished glow of metal from the mine. Or, if metallic, it looked airy and unsubstantial, like the glorified dreams of an alchemist. And speedily—more speedily than in our own clime—came the twilight, and, brightening through its gray transparency, the stars.

A swarm of minute insects that had been hovering all day round the battlements were now swept away by the freshness of a rising breeze. The two owls in the chamber beneath Donatello's uttered their soft, melancholy cry—which, with national avoidance of harsh sounds, Italian owls substitute for the hoot of their kindred in other countries, and flew darkling forth among the shrubbery. A convent-bell rang out, near at hand, and was not only echoed among the hills, but answered by another bell, and still another, which doubtless had farther and farther responses, at various distances along the valley; for, like the English drum-beat around the globe, there is a chain of convent-bells from end to end, and cross-wise, and in all possible directions, over priest-ridden Italy.

"Come," said the sculptor, "the evening air grows cool. It is time to descend."

"Time for you, my friend," replied the count, and he hesitated a little before adding; "I must keep a vigil here for some hours longer. It is my frequent custom to keep vigils; and sometimes the thought occurs to me whether it were not better to keep them in yonder convent, the bell of which just now seemed to summon me. Would I do wisely, do you think, to exchange this old tower for a cell?"

"What! Turn monk?" exclaimed his friend.
"A horrible idea!"

"True," said Donatello, sighing. "Therefore, if at all, I purpose doing it."

"Then think of it no more, for Heaven's sake!" cried the sculptor. "There are a thousand better and more poignant methods of being miserable than that, if to be miserable is what you wish. Nay; I question whether a monk keeps himself up to the intellectual and spiritual height which misery implies. A monk—I judge from their sensual physiognomies, which meet me at every turn—is inevitably a beast! Their souls, if they have any to begin with, perish out of them, before their sluggish, swinish existence is half done. Better, a million times, to stand star-gazing on these airy battlements, than to smother your new germ of a higher life in a monkish cell!"

"You make me tremble," said Donatello, "by your bold aspersion of men who have devoted themselves to God's service!"

"They serve neither God nor man, and themselves least of all, though their motives be utterly selfish," replied Kenyon. "Avoid the convent, my dear friend, as you would shun the death of the soul! But, for my own part, if I had an insupportable burden—if, for any cause, I were bent upon sacrificing every earthly hope as a peace-offering towards heaven—I would make the wide world my cell, and good deeds to mankind my prayer. Many penitent men have done this, and found peace in it."

"Ah! but you are a heretic!" said the count.

Yet his face brightened beneath the stars; and, looking at it through the twilight, the sculptor's remembrance went back to that scene in the Capitol, where, both in features and expression, Donatello had seemed identical with the Faun. And still there was a resemblance; for now, when first the idea was suggested of living for the welfare of his fellow-creatures, the original beauty, which sorrow had partly effaced, came back elevated and spiritualized.

In the black depths, the Faun had found a soul, and was struggling with it towards the light of heaven.

The illumination, it is true, soon faded out of Donatello's face. The idea of life-long and unselfish effort was too high to be received by him with more than a momentary comprehension. An Italian, indeed, seldom dreams of being philanthropic, except in bestowing alms among the paupers, who appeal to his beneficence at every step; nor does it occur to him that there are fitter modes of propitiating Heaven than by penances, pilgrimages, and offerings at shrines. Perhaps, too, their system has its share of moral advantages; they, at all events, cannot well pride themselves, as our own more energetic benevolence is apt to do, upon sharing in the counsels of Providence and kindly helping out its otherwise impracticable designs.

And now the broad valley twinkled with lights, that glimmered through its duskiness, like the fire-flies in the garden of a Florentine palace. A gleam of lightning from the rear of the tempest showed the circumference of hills, and the great space between, as the last cannon-flash of a retreating army reddens across the field where it has fought. The sculptor was on the point of descending the turret-stair, when, somewhere in the darkness that lay beneath them, a woman's voice was heard, singing a low, sad strain.

"Hark!" said he, laying his hand on Donatello's arm.

And Donatello had said "Hark!" at the same instant.

The song, if song it could be called, that had only a wild rhythm, and flowed forth in the fitful measure of a wind-harp, did not clothe itself in the sharp brilliancy of the Italian tongue. The words, so far as they could be distinguished, were German, and therefore unintelligible to the count, and hardly less so to the sculptor; being softened and molten, as it were, into the melancholy richness of the voice that sang them. It was as the murmur of a soul bewildered amid the sinful gloom of earth, and retaining only enough memory of a better state to make sad music of the wail, which would else have been a despairing shriek. Never was there profounder pathos than breathed through that mysterious voice; it brought the tears into the sculptor's eyes, with remembrances and forebodings of whatever sorrow he had felt or apprehended; it made Donatello sob, as chiming in with the anguish that he found unutterable, and giving it the expression which he vaguely sought.

But, when the emotion was at its profoundest depth, the voice rose out of it, yet so gradually that a gloom seemed to pervade it, far upward from the abyss, and not entirely to fall away as it ascended into a higher and purer region. At last, the auditors would have fancied that the melody, with its rich sweetness all there, and much of its sorrow gone, was floating around the very summit of the tower.

"Donatello," said the sculptor, when there was silence again, "had that voice no message for your ear?"

"I dare not receive it," said Donatello; "the anguish of which it spoke abides with me: the hope dies away with the breath that brought it hither. It is not good for me to hear that voice."

The sculptor sighed, and left the poor penitent keeping his vigil on the tower.

CHAPTER XIV.

DONATELLO'S BUST.

KENYON, it will be remembered, had asked Donatello's permission to model his bust. The work had now made considerable progress, and necessarily kept the sculptor's thoughts brooding much and often upon his host's personal characteristics. These it was his difficult office to bring out from their depths, and interpret them to all men, showing them what they could not discern for themselves, yet must be compelled to recognize at a glance, on the surface of a block of marble.

He had never undertaken a portrait-bust which gave him so much trouble as Donatello's; not that there was any special difficulty in hitting the likeness, though even in this respect the grace and harmony of the features seemed inconsistent with a prominent expression of individuality; but he was chiefly perplexed how to make this genial and kindly type of countenance the index of the mind within. His acuteness and his sympathies, indeed, were both somewhat at fault in their efforts to enlighten him as to the moral phase through which the count was now passing. If at one sitting he caught a glimpse of what appeared to be a genuine and permanent trait, it would probably be less perceptible on a second occasion, and perhaps have vanished entirely at a third. So evanescent a show of character threw the sculptor into despair; not marble or clay, but cloud and vapour was the material in which it ought to be represented. Even the ponderous depression which constantly weighed upon Donatello's heart could not compel him into the kind of repose which the plastic art requires.

Hopeless of a good result, Kenyon gave up all preconceptions about the character of his subject, and let his hands work uncontrolled with the clay, somewhat as a spiritual medium, while holding

a pen, yields it to an unseen guidance other than
that of her own will. Now and then he fancied
that his plan was destined to be the successful
one. A skill and insight beyond his consciousness seemed occasionally to take up the task.
The mystery, the miracle, of imbuing an inani-
mate substance with thought, feeling, and all the
intangible attributes of the soul, appeared on the
verge of being wrought. And now, as he flattered
himself, the true image of his friend was about
to emerge from the facile material, bringing with
it more of Donatello's character than the keenest
observer could detect at any one moment in the
face of the original. Vain expectation! some
touch, whereby the artist thought to improve or
hasten the result, interfered with the design of
his unseen spiritual assistant, and spoilt the whole.
There was still the moist, brown clay, indeed,
and the features of Donatello, but without any
semblance of intelligent and sympathetic life.

"The difficulty will drive me mad, I verily
believe!" cried the sculptor, nervously. "Look

at the wretched piece of work yourself, my dear friend, and tell me whether you recognize any manner of likeness to your inner man?"

"None," replied Donatello, speaking the simple truth. "It is like looking a stranger in the face."

This frankly unfavourable testimony so wrought with the sensitive artist, that he fell into a passion with the stubborn image, and cared not what might happen to it thenceforward. Wielding that wonderful power which sculptors possess over moist clay, however, refractory it may show itself in certain respects, he compressed, elongated, widened, and otherwise altered the features of the bust in mere recklessness, and at every change inquired of the count whether the expression became anywise more satisfactory.

"Stop!" cried Donatello at last, catching the sculptor's hand. "Let it remain so!"

By some accidental handling of the clay, entirely independent of his own will, Kenyon had given the countenance a distorted and violent look combining animal fierceness with intelligent hatred. Had Hilda, or had Miriam seen the bust, with the expression which it had now assumed, they might have recognized Donatello's face as they beheld it at that terrible moment, when he held his victim over the edge of the precipice.

"What have I done?" said the sculptor, shocked at his own casual production. "It were a sin to let the clay which bears your features harden into a look like that. Cain never wore an uglier one."

"For that very reason, let it remain!" answered the count, who had grown pale as ashes at the aspect of his crime, thus strangely presented to him in another of the many guises under which guilt stares the criminal in the face. "Do not alter it! Chisel it, rather, in eternal marble! I will set it up in my oratory and keep it continually before my eyes. Sadder and more horrible is a face like this, alive with my own crime, than the dead skull which my forefathers handed down to me!"

But, without in the least heeding Donatello's remonstrances, the sculptor again applied his artful fingers to the clay, and compelled the bust to dismiss the expression that had so startled them both.

"Believe me," said he, turning his eyes upon his friend, full of grave and tender sympathy; "you know not what is requisite for your spiritual growth, seeking, as you do, to keep your soul perpetually in the unwholesome region of remorse. It was needful for you to pass through that dark valley, but it is infinitely dangerous to linger there too long; there is poison in the atmosphere, when we sit down and brood in it, instead of girding up our loins to press onward. Not despondency, not slothful anguish, is what you now require—but effort! Has there been an unutterable evil in your young life? Then crowd it out with good, or it will lie corrupting there for ever, and cause your capacity for better things to partake its noisome corruption!"

"You stir up many thoughts," said Donatello,

pressing his hand upon his brow, "but the multitude and the whirl of them make me dizzy."

They now left the sculptor's temporary studio, without observing that his last accidental touches, with which he hurriedly effaced the look of deadly rage, had given the bust a higher and sweeter expression than it had hitherto worn. It is to be regretted that Kenyon had not seen it; for only an artist, perhaps, can conceive the irksomeness, the irritation of brain, the depression of spirits, that resulted from his failure to satisfy himself, after so much toil and thought as he had bestowed on Donatello's bust. In case of success, indeed, all this thoughtful toil would have been reckoned, not only as well bestowed, but as among the happiest hours of his life; whereas, deeming himself to have failed, it was just so much of life that had better never have been lived; for thus does the good or ill result of his labour throw back sunshine or gloom upon the artist's mind. The sculptor, therefore, would have done well to glance again at his work; for here were still the features of the antique Faun, but now illuminated with a higher meaning, such as the old marble never bore.

Donatello having quitted him, Kenyon spent the rest of the day strolling about the pleasant precincts of Monte Beni, where the summer was now so far advanced that it began, indeed, to partake of the ripe wealth of autumn. Apricots had long been abundant, and had passed away, and plums and cherries along with them. But now came great, juicy pears, melting and delicious, and peaches, of goodly size and tempting aspect, though cold and watery to the palate, compared with the sculptor's rich reminiscences of that fruit in America. The purple figs had already enjoyed their day, and the white ones were luscious now. The contadini (who, by this time, knew Kenyon well) found many clusters of ripe grapes for him, in every little globe of which was included a fragrant draught of the sunny Monte Beni wine.

Unexpectedly, in a nook, close by the farmhouse, he chanced to find a spot where the vintage had actually commenced. A great heap of early ripened grapes had been gathered, and thrown into a mighty tub. In the middle of it stood a lusty and jolly contadino, nor stood merely, but stamped with all his might, and danced amain; while the red juice bathed his feet, and threw its foam midway up his brown and shaggy legs. Here, then, was the very process that figures so picturesquely in Scripture and in poetry, of treading out the wine-press and dyeing the feet and garments with the crimson effusion, as with the blood of a battle-field. . The memory of the process does not make the Tuscan wine taste more deliciously. The contadini hospitably offered Kenyon a sample of the new liquor, that had already stood fermenting for a day or two. He had tried a similar draught, however, in years past, and was little inclined to make proof of it again; for he knew that it would be a sour and bitter juice, a wine of woe and tribulation, and that, the more a man drinks of such liquor, the sadder he is likely to be.

The scene reminded the sculptor of our New England vintages, where the big piles of golden and rosy apples lie under the orchard trees, in the mild, autumnal sunshine; and the creaking cider-mill, set in motion by a circumgyratory horse, is all a-gush with the luscious juice. To speak frankly, the cider-making is the more picturesque sight of the two, and the new sweet cider an infinitely better drink than the ordinary, unripe Tuscan wine. Such as it is, however, the latter fills thousands upon thousands of small, flat barrels, and, still growing thinner and sharper, loses the little life it had as wine, and becomes apotheosized as a more praiseworthy vinegar.

Yet all these vineyard scenes, and the processes connected with the culture of the grape, had a flavour of poetry about them. The toil that produces those kindly gifts of nature which are not the substance of life, but its luxury, is unlike other toil. We are inclined to fancy that it does not bend the sturdy frame, and stiffen the overwrought muscles, like the labour that is devoted in sad, hard earnest, to raise grain for sour bread. Certainly, the sunburnt young men and dark-cheeked, laughing girls, who weeded the rich acres of Monte Beni, might well enough have passed for inhabitants of an unsophisticated Arcadia. Later in the season, when the true vintage-time should come, and the wine of Sunshine gush into the vats, it was hardly too wild a dream that Bacchus himself might revisit the haunts which he loved of old. But, alas, where now would he find the Faun with whom we see him consorting in so many an antique group?

Donatello's remorseful anguish saddened this primitive and delightful life. Kenyon had a pain of his own, moreover, although not all a pain, in the never quiet, never satisfied yearning of his heart towards Hilda. He was authorized to use little freedom towards that shy maiden, even in his visions; so that he almost reproached himself when sometimes his imagination pictured, in detail the sweet years that they might spend together, in a retreat like this. It had just that rarest quality of remoteness from the actual and ordinary world—a remoteness through which all delights might visit them freely, sifted from all troubles which lovers so reasonably insist upon, in their ideal arrangements for a happy union. It is possible, indeed, that even Donatello's grief and Kenyon's pale, sunless affection, lent a charm to Monte Beni, which it would not have retained amid a more redundant joyousness. The sculptor strayed amid its vineyards and orchards, its dells and tangled shrubberies, with somewhat the sensations of an adventurer who should find his way to the site of ancient Eden, and behold its loveliness through the transparency of that gloom which has been brooding over those haunts of innocence ever since the fall. Adam saw it in a brighter sunshine, but never knew the shade of pensive beauty which Eden won from his expulsion.

It was in the decline of the afternoon that Kenyon returned from his long, musing ramble. Old Tomaso—between whom and himself, for some time past, there had been a mysterious understanding—met him in the entrance hall, and drew him a little aside.

"The signorina would speak with you," he whispered.

"In the chapel?" asked the sculptor.

"No; in the saloon beyond it," answered the butler; "the entrance—you once saw the signorina appear through it—is near the altar, hidden behind the tapestry."

Kenyon lost no time in obeying the summons.

CHAPTER XV.

THE MARBLE SALOON.

In an old Tuscan villa, a chapel ordinarily makes one among the numerous apartments; though it often happens that the door is permanently closed, the key lost, and the place left to itself, in dusty sanctity, like that chamber in man's heart where he hides his religious awe. This was very much the case with the chapel of Monte Beni. One rainy day, however, in his wanderings through the great, intricate house, Kenyon had unexpectedly found his way into it, and been impressed by its solemn aspect. The arched windows, high upward in the wall, and darkened with dust and cobweb, threw down a dim light that showed the altar, with a picture of a martyrdom above, and some tall tapers ranged before it. They had apparently been lighted, and burned an hour or two, and been extinguished perhaps half a century before. The marble vase at the entrance held some hardened mud at the bottom, accruing from the dust that had settled in it during the gradual evaporation of the holy water; and a spider (being an insect that delights in pointing the moral of desolation and neglect) had taken pains to weave a prodigiously thick tissue across the circular brim. An old family banner, tattered by the moths, drooped from the vaulted roof. In niches, there were some mediæval busts of Donatello's forgotten ancestry; and among them, it might be, the forlorn visage of that hapless knight, between whom and the fountain-nymph had occurred such tender love passages.

Throughout all the jovial prosperity of Monte Beni, this one spot within the domestic walls had kept itself silent, stern, and sad. When the individual or the family retired from song and mirth, they here sought those realities which men do not invite their festive associates to share. And here, on the occasion above referred to, the sculptor had discovered—accidentally, so far as he was concerned, though with a purpose on her part—that there was a guest under Donatello's roof, whose presence the count did not suspect. An interview had since taken place, and he was now summoned to another.

He crossed the chapel, in compliance with Tomaso's instructions, and, passing through the side entrance, found himself in a saloon, of no great size, but more magnificent than he had supposed the villa to contain. As it was vacant, Kenyon had leisure to pace it once or twice, and examine it with a careless sort of scrutiny, before any person appeared.

This beautiful hall was floored with rich marbles, in artistically arranged figures and compartments. The walls, likewise, were almost entirely cased in marble of various kinds, the prevalent variety being giallo antico, intermixed with verde antique, and others equally precious. The splendour of the giallo antico, however, was what gave character to the saloon; and the large and deep niches, apparently intended for full-length statues, along the walls, were lined with the same costly material. Without visiting Italy, one can have no idea of the beauty and magnificence that are produced by these fittings-up of polished marble. Without such experience, indeed, we do not even know what marble means, in any sense, save as the white limestone of which we carve our mantel-pieces. This rich hall of Monte Beni, moreover, was adorned, at its upper end, with two pillars that seemed to consist of oriental alabaster; and wherever there was a space vacant of precious and variegated marble, it was frescoed with ornaments in arabesque. Above, there was a coved and vaulted ceiling, glowing with pictured scenes, which affected Kenyon with a vague sense of splendour, without his twisting his neck to gaze at them.

It is one of the special excellences of such a saloon of polished and richly coloured marble, that decay can never tarnish it. Until the house crumbles down upon it, it shines indestructibly, and with a little dusting looks just as brilliant in its three hundredth year, as the day after the final slab of giallo antico was fitted into the wall. To the sculptor, at this first view of it, it seemed a hall where the sun was magically imprisoned, and must always shine. He anticipated Miriam's entrance, arrayed in queenly robes, and beaming with even more than the singular beauty that had heretofore distinguished her.

While this thought was passing through his mind, the pillared door, at the upper end of the saloon, was partly opened, and Miriam appeared. She was very pale, and dressed in deep mourning. As she advanced towards the sculptor, the feebleness of her step was so apparent that he made haste to meet her, apprehending that she might sink down on the marble floor, without the instant support of his arm.

But, with a gleam of her natural self-reliance, she declined his aid, and, after touching her cold hand to his, went and sat down on one of the cushioned divans that were ranged against the wall.

"You are very ill, Miriam!" said Kenyon, much shocked at her appearance. "I had not thought of this."

"No; not so ill as I seem to you," she answered, adding despondently, "yet I am ill enough, I believe, to die, unless some change speedily occurs."

"What, then, is your disorder?" asked the sculptor; "and what the remedy?"

"The disorder!" repeated Miriam. "There is none that I know of, save too much life and strength, without a purpose for one or the other. It is my too redundant energy that is slowly—or perhaps rapidly—wearing me away, because I can apply it to no use. The object, which I am bound to consider my only one on earth, fails me utterly. The sacrifice which I yearn to make of myself, my hopes, my everything, is coldly put aside. Nothing is left for me but to brood, brood, brood, all day, all night, in unprofitable longings and repinings.

"This is very sad, Miriam," said Kenyon.

"Ay, indeed; I fancy so," she replied, with a short, unnatural laugh.

"With all your activity of mind," resumed he, "so fertile in plans as I have known you, can you imagine no method of bringing your resources into play?"

"My mind is not active any longer," answered Miriam, in a cold, indifferent tone. "It deals with one thought and no more. One recollection paralyzes it. It is not remorse; do not think it! I put myself out of the question, and feel neither regret nor penitence on my own behalf. But what benumbs me—what robs me of all power—it is no secret for a woman to tell a man, yet I care not though you know it—is the certainty that I am, and must ever be, an object of horror in Donatello's sight."

The sculptor—a young man, and cherishing

a love which insulated him from the wild experiences which some men gather—was startled to perceive how Miriam's rich, ill-regulated nature impelled her to fling herself, conscience and all, on one passion, the object of which intellectually seemed far beneath her.

"How have you obtained the certainty of which you speak?" asked he, after a pause.

"Oh, by a sure token," said Miriam, "a gesture, merely; a shudder, a cold shiver that ran through him one sunny morning when his hand happened to touch mine! But it was enough."

"I firmly believe, Miriam," said the sculptor, "that he loves you still."

She started, and a flush of colour came tremulously over the paleness of her cheek.

"Yes," repeated Kenyon, "if my interest in Donatello and in yourself, Miriam, endows me with any true insight, he not only loves you still, but with a force and depth proportioned to the stronger grasp of his faculties, in their new development."

"Do not deceive me," said Miriam, growing pale again.

"Not for the world!" replied Kenyon. "Here is what I take to be the truth. There was an interval, no doubt, when the horror of some calamity, which I need not shape out in my conjectures, threw Donatello into a stupor of misery. Connected with the first shock there was an intolerable pain and shuddering repugnance attaching themselves to all the circumstances and surroundings of the event that so terribly affected him. Was his dearest friend involved within the horror of that moment, he would shrink from her, as he shrank most of all from himself. But, as his mind roused itself—as it rose to a higher life than he had hitherto experienced—whatever had been true and permanent within him revived by the selfsame impulse. So has it been with his love."

"But, surely," said Miriam, "he knows that I am here! Why, then, except that I am odious to him, does he not bid me welcome?"

"He is, I believe, aware of your presence here," answered the sculptor. "Your song, a night or two ago, must have revealed it to him; and, in truth, I had fancied that there was already a consciousness of it in his mind. But, the more passionately he longs for your society, the more religiously he deems himself bound to avoid it. The idea of a life-long penance has taken strong possession of Donatello. He gropes blindly about him for some method of sharp self-torture, and finds, of course, no other so efficacious as this."

"But he loves me," repeated Miriam, in a low voice, to herself. "Yes; he loves me!"

It was strange to observe the womanly softness that came over her, as she admitted that comfort into her bosom. The cold, unnatural indifference of her manner, a kind of frozen passionateness, which had shocked and chilled the sculptor, disappeared. She blushed, and turned away her eyes, knowing that there was more surprise and joy in their dewy glances, than any man save one ought to detect there.

"In other respects," she inquired at length, "is he much changed?"

"A wonderful process is going forward in Donatello's mind," answered the sculptor. "The germs of faculties that have heretofore slept are fast springing into activity. The world of thought is disclosing itself to his inward sight. He startles me, at times, with his perception of deep truths; and, quite as often, it must be owned, he compels me to smile by the intermixture of his former simplicity with a new intelligence. But, he is bewildered with the revelations that each day brings. Out of his bitter agony, a soul and intellect, I could almost say, have been inspired into him."

"Ah, I could help him here!" cried Miriam, clasping her hands. "And how sweet a toil to bend and adapt my whole nature to do him good! To instruct, to elevate, to enrich his mind with the wealth that would flow in upon me, had I such a motive for acquiring it! Who else can perform the task? Who else has the tender sympathy which he requires? Who else, save only me—a woman, a sharer in the same dread secret, a partaker in one identical guilt—could meet him on such terms of intimate equality as the case demands? With this object before me, I might feel a right to live! Without it, it is a shame for me to have lived so long."

"I fully agree with you," said Kenyon, "that your true place is by his side."

"Surely it is," replied Miriam. "If Donatello is entitled to aught on earth, it is to my complete self-sacrifice for his sake. It does not weaken his claim, methinks, that my only prospect of happiness—a fearful word, however—lies in the good that may accrue to him from our intercourse. But he rejects me! He will not listen to the whisper of his heart, telling him that she, most wretched, who beguiled him into evil, might guide him to a higher innocence than that from which he fell. How is this first, great difficulty to be obviated?"

"It lies at your own option, Miriam, to do

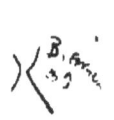

away the obstacle, at any moment," remarked the sculptor. "It is but to ascend Donatello's tower, and you will meet him there, under the eye of God."

"I dare not," answered Miriam. "No; I dare not!"

"Do you fear," asked the sculptor, "the dread eye-witness whom I have named?"

"No; for, as far as I can see into that cloudy and inscrutable thing, my heart, it has none but pure motives," replied Miriam. "But, my friend, you little know what a weak, or what a strong creature, a woman is! I fear not Heaven, in this case at least, but—shall I confess it?—I am greatly in dread of Donatello. Once, he shuddered at my touch. If he shudder once again, or frown, I die!"

Kenyon could not but marvel at the subjection into which this proud and self-dependent woman had wilfully flung herself, hanging her life upon the chance of an angry or favourable regard from a person who, a little while before, had seemed the plaything of a moment. But, in Miriam's eyes, Donatello was always, thenceforth, invested with the tragic dignity of their hour of crime; and, furthermore, the keen and deep insight, with which her love endowed her, enabled her to know him far better than he could be known by ordinary observation. Beyond all question, since she loved him so, there was a force in Donatello worthy of her respect and love.

"You see my weakness," said Miriam, flinging out her hands, as a person does when a defect is acknowledged, and beyond remedy. "What I need, now, is an opportunity to show my strength."

"It has occurred to me," Kenyon remarked, "that the time is come, when it may be desirable to remove Donatello from the complete seclusion in which he buries himself. He has struggled long enough with one idea. He now needs a variety of thought, which cannot be otherwise so readily supplied to him, as through the medium of a variety of scenes. His mind is awakened

now; his heart, though full of pain, is no longer
benumbed. They should have food and solace.
If he linger here much longer, I fear that he may
sink back into a lethargy. The extreme excita-
bility, which circumstances have imparted to his
moral system, has its dangers and its advantages;
it being one of the dangers, that an obdurate
scar may supervene upon its very tenderness.
Solitude has done what it could for him; now,
for a while, let him be enticed into the outer
world."

"What is your plan, then?" asked Miriam.

"Simply," replied Kenyon, "to persuade Donatello to be my companion in a ramble among
these hills and valleys. The little adventures and
vicissitudes of travel will do him infinite good.
After his recent profound experience, he will
re-create the world by the new eyes with which
he will regard it. He will escape, I hope, out
of a morbid life, and find his way into a healthy
one."

"And what is to be my part in this process?"

inquired Miriam, sadly, and not without jealousy. "You are taking him from me, and putting yourself, and all manner of living interests, into the place which I ought to fill!"

"It would rejoice me, Miriam, to yield the entire responsibility of this office to yourself," answered the sculptor. "I do not pretend to be the guide and counsellor whom Donatello needs; for, to mention no other obstacle, I am a man, and between man and man there is always an insuperable gulf. They can never quite grasp each other's hands; and therefore man never derives any intimate help, any heart sustenance, from his brother man, but from woman— his mother, his sister, or his wife. Be Donatello's friend at need, therefore, and most gladly will I resign him!"

"It is not kind to taunt me thus," said Miriam. "I have told you that I cannot do what you suggest, because I dare not."

"Well, then," rejoined the sculptor, "see if there is any possibility of adapting yourself to

my scheme. The incidents of a journey often
fling people together in the oddest, and therefore
the most natural way. Supposing you were to
find yourself on the same route, a reunion with
Donatello might ensue, and Providence have a
larger hand in it than either of us."

"It is not a hopeful plan," said Miriam,
shaking her head, after a moment's thought;
"yet I will not reject it without a trial. Only,
in case it fail, here is a resolution to which I
bind myself, come what come may! You know
the bronze statue of Pope Julius, in the great
square of Perugia? I remember standing in the
shadow of that statue, one sunny noontime, and
being impressed by its paternal aspect, and fancying that a blessing fell upon me from its out-
stretched hand. Ever since, I have had a superstition—you will call it foolish, but sad and
ill-fated persons always dream such things—that,
if I waited long enough in that same spot, some
good event would come to pass. Well, my friend,
precisely a fortnight after you begin your tour

unless we sooner meet—bring Donatello, at noon, to the base of the statue. You will find me there!"

Kenyon assented to the proposed arrangement, and, after some conversation respecting his contemplated line of travel, prepared to take his leave. As he met Miriam's eyes, in bidding farewell, he was surprised at the new, tender gladness that beamed out of them, and at the appearance of health and bloom, which, in this little while, had overspread her face.

"May I tell you, Miriam," said he, smiling, "that you are still as beautiful as ever?"

"You have a right to notice it," she replied, "for, if it be so, my faded bloom has been revived by the hopes you give me. Do you, then, think me beautiful? I rejoice, most truly. Beauty—if I possess it—shall be one of the instruments by which I will try to educate and elevate him, to whose good I solely dedicate myself."

The sculptor had nearly reached the door,

when, hearing her call him, he turned back, and
beheld Miriam still standing where he had left
her, in the magnificent hall which seemed only
a fit setting for her beauty. She beckoned him
to return.

"You are a man of refined taste," said she;
"more than that—a man of delicate sensibility.
Now tell me frankly, and on your honour,
have I not shocked you many times during this
interview, by my betrayal of woman's cause, my
lack of feminine modesty, my reckless, passionate,
most indecorous avowal, that I live only in the
life of one who perhaps scorns and shudders
at me?"

Thus adjured, however difficult the point
to which she brought him, the sculptor was
not a man to swerve aside from the simple
truth.

"Miriam," replied he, "you exaggerate the
impression made upon my mind; but it has been
painful, and somewhat of the character which you
suppose."

"I knew it," said Miriam, mournfully, but with no resentment. "What remains of my finer nature would have told me so, even if it had not been perceptible in all your manner. Well, my dear friend, when you go back to Rome, tell Hilda what her severity has done! She was all Womanhood to me; and when she cast me off, I had no longer any terms to keep with the reserves and decorums of my sex. Hilda has set me free! Pray tell her so, from Miriam, and thank her!"

"I shall tell Hilda nothing that will give her pain," answered Kenyon. "But, Miriam, though I know not what passed between her and yourself—I feel—and let the noble frankness of your disposition forgive me, if I say so—I feel that she was right. You have a thousand admirable qualities. Whatever mass of evil may have fallen into your life—pardon me, but your own words suggest it—you are still as capable as ever of many high and heroic virtues. But the white shining purity of Hilda's nature is a thing apart;

and she is bound, by the undefiled material of which God moulded her, to keep that severity which I, as well as you, have recognized."

"Oh, you are right!" said Miriam; "I never questioned it; though, as I told you, when she cast me off, it severed some few remaining bonds between me and decorous womanhood. But were there anything to forgive, I do forgive her. May you win her virgin heart; for methinks there can be few men in this evil world who are not more unworthy of her than yourself."

CHAPTER XVI.

SCENES BY THE WAY.

When it came to the point of quitting the reposeful life of Monte Beni, the sculptor was not without regrets, and would willingly have dreamed a little longer of the sweet paradise on earth that Hilda's presence there might make. Nevertheless, amid all its repose, he had begun to be sensible of a restless melancholy, to which the cultivators of the ideal arts are more liable than sturdier men. On his own part, therefore, and leaving Donatello out of the case, he would have judged it well to go. He made parting visits to the legendary dell, and to other delightful spots with which he had grown familiar; he climbed the tower again, and saw a sunset and a moonrise over the great valley; he drank, on the eve of his departure, one flask, and then another, of the Monte Beni Sunshine, and stored up its flavour in his memory, as the standard of what is exquisite in wine. These things accomplished, Kenyon was ready for the journey.

Donatello had not very easily been stirred out of the peculiar sluggishness, which enthrals and bewitches melancholy people. He had offered merely a passive resistance, however, not an active one, to his friend's schemes; and when the appointed hour came, he yielded to the impulse which Kenyon failed not to apply; and was started upon the journey, before he had made up his mind to undertake it. They wandered forth at large, like two knights-errant, among the valleys, and the mountains, and the old mountain-towns of that picturesque and lovely region. Save to keep the appointment with Miriam, a fortnight thereafter, in the great square of Perugia, there was nothing more definite in the sculptor's plan, than that they should let themselves be blown hither and thither like winged seeds, that mount upon each wandering breeze. Yet there was an idea of fatality implied in the simile of the winged seeds, which did not altogether suit Kenyon's fancy; for, if you look closely into the matter, it will be seen that whatever appears most vagrant, and utterly purposeless, turns out, in the end, to have been impelled the most surely on a pre-ordained and unswerving track. Chance and change love to deal with men's settled plans, not with their idle vagaries. If we desire unexpected and unimaginable events, we should contrive an iron framework, such as we fancy may compel the future to take one inevitable shape; then comes in the Unexpected, and shatters our design in fragments.

The travellers set forth on horseback, and purposed to perform much of their aimless journeyings, under the moon, and in the cool of the morning or evening twilight; the mid-day sun, while summer had hardly begun to trail its

departing skirts over Tuscany, being still too
fervid to allow of noontide exposure.

For a while, they wandered in that same broad
valley which Kenyon had viewed with such
delight from the Monte Beni tower. The sculptor
soon began to enjoy the idle activity of their new
life, which the lapse of a day or two sufficed
to establish as a kind of system; it is so natural
for mankind to be nomadic, that a very little taste
of that primitive mode of existence subverts the
settled habits of many preceding years. Kenyon's cares, and whatever gloomy ideas before
possessed him, seemed to be left at Monte Beni,
and were scarcely remembered by the time that
its gray tower grew indistinguishable on the
brown hill-side. His perceptive faculties, which
had found little exercise of late, amid so thoughtful a way of life, became keen, and kept his
eyes busy with a hundred agreeable scenes.

He delighted in the picturesque bits of rustic
character and manners, so little of which ever

comes upon the surface of our life at home. There, for example, were the old women, tending pigs or sheep by the wayside. As they followed the vagrant steps of their charge, these venerable ladies kept spinning yarn with that elsewhere forgotten contrivance, the distaff; and so wrinkled and stern-looking were they, that you might have taken them for the Parcæ, spinning the threads of human destiny. In contrast with their great-grandmothers were the children, leading goats of shaggy beard, tied by the horns, and letting them browse on branch and shrub. It is the fashion of Italy to add the petty industry of age and childhood to the sum of human toil. To the eyes of an observer from the western world, it was a strange spectacle to see sturdy, sunburnt creatures, in petticoats, but otherwise manlike, toiling side by side with male labourers, in the rudest work of the fields. These sturdy women (if as such we must recognize them) wore the high-crowned, broad-brimmed hat of Tuscan straw, the customary female head-apparel;

and, as every breeze blew back its breadth of
brim, the sunshine constantly added depth to the
brown glow of their cheeks. The elder sisterhood, however, set off their witch-like ugliness
to the worst advantage with black felt hats,
bequeathed them, one would fancy, by their long-
buried husbands.

Another ordinary sight, as sylvan as the above,
and more agreeable, was a girl, bearing on her
back a huge bundle of green twigs and shrubs,
or grass, intermixed with scarlet poppies and
blue flowers; the verdant burden being sometimes of such size as to hide the bearer's figure,
and seem a self-moving mass of fragrant bloom
and verdure. Oftener, however, the bundle
reached only half-way down the back of the
rustic nymph, leaving in sight her well-developed
lower limbs, and the crooked knife, hanging
behind her, with which she had been reaping
this strange harvest sheaf. A pre-Raphaelite
artist (he, for instance, who painted so marvel-
lously a wind-swept heap of autumnal leaves)

might find an admirable subject in one of these
Tuscan girls, stepping with a free, erect, and
graceful carriage. The miscellaneous herbage and
tangled twigs and blossoms of her bundle, crowning
her head (while her ruddy, comely face looks out
between the hanging side festoons like a larger
flower), would give the painter boundless scope for
the minute delineation which he loves.

Though mixed up with what was rude and
earthlike, there was still a remote, dreamlike,
Arcadian charm, which is scarcely to be found
in the daily toil of other lands. Among the
pleasant features of the wayside were always
the vines, clambering on fig-trees, or other
sturdy trunks; they wreathed themselves, in
huge and rich festoons, from one tree to another,
suspending clusters of ripening grapes in the
interval between. Under such careless mode of
culture, the luxuriant vine is a lovelier spectacle
than where it produces a more precious liquor,
and is therefore more artificially restrained and
trimmed. Nothing can be more picturesque than

an old grape-vine, with almost a trunk of its own, clinging fast around its supporting tree. Nor does the picture lack its moral. You might twist it to more than one grave purpose, as you saw how the knotted, serpentine growth imprisoned within its strong embrace the friend that had supported its tender infancy; and how (as seemingly flexible natures are prone to do) it converted the sturdier tree entirely to its own selfish ends, extending its innumerable arms on every bough, and permitting hardly a leaf to sprout except its own. It occurred to Kenyon, that the enemies of the vine, in his native land, might here have seen an emblem of the remorseless gripe which the habit of vinous enjoyment lays upon its victim, possessing him wholly, and letting him live no life but such as it bestows.

The scene was not less characteristic when their path led the two wanderers through some small ancient town. There, besides the peculiarities of present life, they saw tokens of the life that had long ago been lived and flung aside. The little town, such as we see in our mind's eye, would have its gate and its surrounding walls, so ancient and massive that ages had not sufficed to crumble them away; but in the lofty upper portion of the gateway, still standing over the empty arch, where there was no longer a gate to shut, there would be a dovecote, and peaceful doves for the only warders. Pumpkins lay ripening in the open chambers of the structure. Then, as for the town-wall, on the outside an orchard extends peacefully along its base, full, not of apple-trees, but of those old humorists with gnarled trunks and twisted boughs, the olives. Houses have been built upon the ramparts, or burrowed out of their ponderous foundation. Even the gray, martial towers, crowned with ruined turrets, have been converted into rustic habitations, from the windows of which hang ears of Indian corn. At a door, that has been broken through the massive stone-work, where it was meant to be strongest, some contadini are winnowing grain. Small windows, too, are pierced through the whole line of ancient wall, so that it seems a row of dwellings with one continuous front, built in a strange style of needless strength; but remnants of the old battlements and machicolations are interspersed with the homely chambers and earthen-tiled house-tops; and all along its extent both grape-vines and running flower-shrubs are encouraged to clamber and sport over the roughnesses of its decay.

Finally, the long grass, intermixed with weeds and wild-flowers, waves on the uppermost height of the shattered rampart; and it is exceedingly pleasant in the golden sunshine of the afternoon, to behold the warlike precinct so friendly in its old days, and so overgrown with rural peace. In its guard-rooms, its prison chambers, and scooped out of its ponderous breadth, there are dwellings now-a-days where happy human lives are spent. Human parents and broods of children nestle in them, even as the swallows nestle in the little crevices along the broken summit of the wall.

SCENES BY THE WAY.

Passing through the gateway of this same little town, challenged only by those watchful sentinels, the pigeons, we find ourselves in a long narrow street, paved from side to side with flag-stones, in the old Roman fashion. Nothing can exceed the grim ugliness of the houses, most of which are three or four stories high, stone-built, gray, dilapidated, or half covered with plaster in patches, and contiguous all along from end to end of the town. Nature, in the shape of tree, shrub, or grassy side-walk, is as much shut out from the one street of the rustic village as from the heart of any swarming city. The dark and half-ruinous habitations, with their small windows, many of which are drearily closed with wooden shutters, are but magnified hovels, piled story upon story, and squalid with the grime that successive ages have left behind them. It would be a hideous scene to contemplate in a rainy day, or when no human life pervaded it. In the summer-noon, however, it possesses vivacity enough to keep itself cheerful; for all the within-doors of the village then bubbles over upon the flag-stones, or looks out from the small windows, and from here and there a balcony. Some of the populace are at the butcher's shop; others are at the fountain, which gushes into a marble basin that resembles an antique sarcophagus. A tailor is sewing before his door, with a young priest seated sociably beside him; a burly friar goes by with an empty wine-barrel on his head; children are at play; women at their own doorsteps mend clothes, embroider, weave hats of Tuscan straw, or twirl the distaff. Many idlers, meanwhile, strolling from one group to another, let the warm day slide by in the sweet, interminable task of doing nothing.

From all these people there comes a babblement that seems quite disproportioned to the number of tongues that make it. So many words are not uttered in a New England village throughout the year, except it be at a political caucus or town-meeting, as are spoken here, with no especial purpose, in a single day. Neither so many words, nor so much laughter; for people talk about nothing as if they were terribly in earnest, and make merry at nothing, as if it were the best of all possible jokes. In so long a time as they have existed, and within such narrow precincts, these little walled towns are brought into a closeness of society that makes them but a larger household. All the inhabitants are akin to each, and each to all; they assemble in the street as their common saloon, and thus live and die in a familiarity of intercourse, such as never can be known where a village is open at either end, and all roundabout, and has ample room within itself.

Stuck up beside the door of one house, in this village street, is a withered bough; and, on a stone seat, just under the shadow of the bough, sits a party of jolly drinkers, making proof of the new wine, or quaffing the old, as their often-tried and comfortable friend. Kenyon draws bridle here, (for the bough, or bush, is a symbol of the wine-shop at this day in Italy, as it was three hundred years ago in England) and calls for a goblet of the deep, mild purple juice, well diluted with water from the fountain. The Sunshine of Monte Beni would be welcome now. Meanwhile, Donatello has ridden onward, but alights where a shrine, with a burning lamp before it, is built into the wall of an inn-stable. He kneels, and crosses himself, and mutters a brief prayer, without attracting notice from the passers-by; many of whom are parenthetically devout, in a similar fashion. By this time the sculptor has drunk off his wine-and-water, and our two travellers resume their way, emerging from the opposite gate of the village.

Before them, again, lies the broad valley, with a mist so thinly scattered over it as to be perceptible only in the distance, and most so in the nooks of the hills. Now that we have called it mist, it seems a mistake not rather to have called it sunshine; the glory of so much

light being mingled with so little gloom, in
the airy material of that vapour. Be it mist
or sunshine, it adds a touch of ideal beauty to
the scene, almost persuading the spectator that
this valley and those hills are visionary, because their visible atmosphere is so like the
substance of a dream.

Immediately about them, however, there were
abundant tokens that the country was not really
the paradise it looked to be, at a casual glance.
Neither the wretched cottages nor the dreary
farmhouses seemed to partake of the prosperity,
with which so kindly a climate, and so fertile
a portion of Mother Earth's bosom, should have
filled them, one and all. But, possibly, the
peasant inhabitants do not exist in so grimy a
poverty, and in homes so comfortless, as a
stranger, with his native ideas of those matters,
would be likely to imagine. The Italians appear to possess none of that emulative pride
which we see in our New England villages,
where every householder, according to his taste

and means, endeavours to make his homestead an ornament to the grassy and elm-shadowed wayside. In Italy there are no neat doorsteps and thresholds; no pleasant, vine-sheltered porches; none of those grass-plots or smoothly shorn lawns, which hospitably invite the imagination into the sweet domestic interiors of English life. Everything, however sunny and luxuriant may be the scene around, is especially disheartening in the immediate neighbourhood of an Italian home.

An artist, it is true, might often thank his stars for those old houses, so picturesquely time-stained, and with the plaster falling in blotches from the ancient brickwork. The prison-like, iron-barred windows, and the wide-arched, dismal entrance, admitting on one hand to the stable, on the other to the kitchen, might impress him as far better worth his pencil than the newly painted pine boxes, in which—if he be an American—his countrymen live and thrive. But there is reason to suspect that a people are waning to decay and ruin the moment that their life becomes fascinating either in the poet's imagination or the painter's eye.

As usual on Italian waysides, the wanderers passed great black crosses, hung with all the instruments of the sacred agony and passion; there were the crown of thorns, the hammer and nails, the pincers, the spear, the sponge, and perched over the whole, the cock that crowed to Saint Peter's remorseful conscience. Thus, while the fertile scene showed the never-failing beneficence of the Creator towards man in his transitory state, these symbols reminded each wayfarer of the Saviour's infinitely greater love for him as an immortal spirit. Beholding these consecrated stations, the idea seemed to strike Donatello of converting the otherwise aimless journey into a penitential pilgrimage. At each of them he alighted to kneel and kiss the cross, and humbly press his forehead against its foot; and this so invariably, that the sculptor soon learned to draw bridle of his own accord. It may be, too, heretic as he was, that Kenyon likewise put up a prayer, rendered more fervent by the symbols before his eyes, for the peace of his friend's conscience, and the pardon of the sin that so oppressed him.

Not only at the crosses did Donatello kneel, but at each of the many shrines, where the blessed Virgin in fresco—faded with sunshine and half washed out with showers—looked benignly at her worshipper; or where she was represented in a wooden image, or a bas-relief of plaster or marble, as accorded with the means of the devout person who built, or restored from a mediæval antiquity, these places of wayside worship. They were everywhere; under arched niches, or in little pent-houses with a brick tiled roof, just large enough to shelter them; or perhaps in some bit of old Roman masonry, the founders of which had died before the Advent; or in the wall of a country inn or farmhouse, or at the midway point of a bridge, or in the shallow cavity of a natural rock, or high upward in the deep cuts of the road. It appeared to the sculptor that Donatello prayed the more earnestly and the more hopefully at these shrines, because the mild face of the Madonna promised him to intercede, as a tender mother, betwixt the poor culprit and the awfulness of judgment.

It was beautiful to observe, indeed, how tender was the soul of man and woman towards the Virgin mother, in recognition of the tenderness which, as their faith taught them, she immortally cherishes towards all human souls. In the wire-work screen, before each shrine, hung offerings of roses, or whatever flower was sweetest and most seasonable; some already wilted and withered, some fresh with that very morning's dewdrops. Flowers there were, too, that, being artificial, never bloomed on earth, nor would ever fade. The thought occurred to Kenyon, that flower-pots with living plants might be set within the niches, or even that rose-trees, and all kinds of flowering shrubs, might be reared under the shrines and taught to twine and wreath themselves around; so that the Virgin should dwell within a bower of verdure, bloom, and fragrant freshness, symbolizing a homage perpetually new. There are many things in the religious customs of these people that seem good; many things, at least, that might be both good and beautiful, if the soul of goodness and the sense of beauty were as much alive in the Italians now as they must have been when those customs were first imagined and adopted. But, instead of blossoms on the shrub, or freshly gathered, with the dewdrops on their leaves, their worship, now-a-days, is best symbolized by the artificial flower.

The sculptor fancied, moreover (but perhaps it was his heresy that suggested the idea), that it would be of happy influence to place a comfortable and shady seat beneath every wayside shrine. Then, the weary and sun-scorched traveller, while resting himself under her protecting shadow, might thank the Virgin for her hospitality. Nor, perchance, were he to regale himself, even in such a consecrated spot, with the fragrance of a pipe, would it rise to heaven more offensively than the smoke of priestly incense. We do ourselves wrong, and too meanly estimate the Holiness above us, when we deem that any act or enjoyment, good in itself, is not good to do religiously.

Whatever may be the iniquities of the papal system, it was a wise and lovely sentiment, that set up the frequent shrine and cross along the roadside. No wayfarer, bent on whatever worldly errand, can fail to be reminded, at every mile or two, that this is not the business which most concerns him. The pleasure-seeker is silently admonished to look heavenward for a joy infinitely greater than he now possesses. The wretch in temptation beholds the cross, and is warned, that if he yield, the Saviour's agony for his sake will have been endured in vain. The stubborn criminal, whose heart has long been like a stone, feels it throb anew with dread and hope; and our poor Donatello, as he went kneeling from shrine to cross, and from cross to shrine, doubtless found an efficacy in these symbols that helped him towards a higher penitence.

Whether the young Count of Monte Beni noticed the fact, or no, there was more than one incident of their journey that led Kenyon to believe, that they were attended, or closely followed, or preceded, near at hand, by some one who took an interest in their motions. As it were, the step, the sweeping garment, the faintly-heard breath, of an invisible companion, was beside them, as they went on their way. It was like a dream that had strayed out of their slumber and was haunting them in the daytime, when its shadowy substance could have neither density nor outline, in the too obtrusive light. After sunset, it grew a little more distinct.

"On the left of that last shrine," asked the sculptor, as they rode, under the moon, "did you observe the figure of a woman kneeling, with her face hidden in her hands?"

"I never looked that way," replied Donatello. "I was saying my own prayer. It was some penitent, perchance. May the Blessed Virgin be the more gracious to the poor soul, because she is a woman."

CHAPTER XVII.

PICTURED WINDOWS.

AFTER wide wanderings through the valley, the two travellers directed their course towards its boundary of hills. Here, the natural scenery and men's modifications of it immediately took a different aspect from that of the fertile and smiling plain. Not unfrequently there was a convent on the hillside; or, on some insulated promontory, a ruined castle, once the den of a robber chieftain, who was accustomed to dash down from his commanding height upon the road that wound below. For ages back, the old fortress had been flinging down its crumbling ramparts, stone by stone, towards the grimy village at its foot.

Their road wound onward among the hills,

which rose steep and lofty from the scanty level space that lay between them. They continually thrust their great bulks before the wayfarers, as if grimly resolute to forbid their passage, or closed abruptly behind them, when they still dared to proceed. A gigantic hill would set its foot right down before them, and only at the last moment would grudgingly withdraw it, just far enough to let them creep towards another obstacle. Adown these rough heights were visible the dry tracks of many a mountain-torrent, that had lived a life too fierce and passionate to be a long one. Or, perhaps a stream was yet hurrying shyly along the edge of a far wider bed of pebbles and shelving rock than it seemed to need, though not too wide for the swollen rage of which this shy rivulet was capable. A stone bridge bestrode it, the ponderous arches of which were upheld and rendered indestructible by the weight of the very stones that threatened to crush them down. Old Roman toil was perceptible in the foundations of that massive bridge; the first weight that it ever bore was that of an army of the Republic.

Threading these defiles, they would arrive at some immemorial city, crowning the high summit of a hill with its cathedral, its many churches, and public edifices, all of Gothic architecture. With no more level ground than a single piazza in the midst, the ancient town tumbled its crooked and narrow streets down the mountain side, through arched passages and by steps of stone. The aspect of everything was awfully old; older, indeed, in its effect on the imagination, than Rome itself, because history does not lay its finger on these forgotten edifices and tell us all about their origin. Etruscan princes may have dwelt in them. A thousand years, at all events, would seem but a middle age for these structures. They are built of such huge, square stones, that their appearance of ponderous durability distresses the beholder with the idea that they can never fall—never crumble away—never be less fit than now for human habitation. Many of them may once have been palaces, and still retain a squalid grandeur. But, gazing at them, we recognize how undesirable it is to build the tabernacle of our brief lifetime out of permanent materials, and with a view to their being occupied by future generations.

All towns should be made capable of purification by fire, or of decay within each half-century. Otherwise, they become the hereditary haunts of vermin and noisomeness, besides standing apart from the possibility of such improvements as are constantly introduced into the rest of man's contrivances and accommodations. It is beautiful, no doubt, and exceedingly satisfactory to some of our natural instincts, to imagine our far posterity dwelling under the same roof-tree as ourselves. Still, when people insist on building indestructible houses, they incur, or their children do, a misfortune analogous to that of the Sibyl, when she obtained the grievous boon of immortality. So, we may build almost immortal habitations, it is true; but we cannot keep them from growing old, musty, unwholesome, dreary, full of death-scents, ghosts, and murder-stains; in short, habitations such as one sees everywhere in Italy, be they hovels or palaces.

"You should go with me to my native country," observed the sculptor to Donatello. "In that fortunate land, each generation has only its own sins and sorrows to bear. Here, it seems as if all the weary and dreary Past were piled upon the back of the Present. If I were to lose my spirits in this country—if I were to suffer any heavy misfortune here—methinks it would be impossible to stand up against it, under such adverse influences."

"The sky itself is an old roof, now," answered the count; "and, no doubt, the sins of mankind have made it gloomier than it used to be."

"Oh, my poor Faun," thought Kenyon to himself, "how art thou changed!"

A city, like this of which we speak, seems a sort of stony growth out of the hill-side, or a fossilized town; so ancient and strange it looks, without enough of life and juiciness in it to be any longer susceptible of decay. An earthquake would afford it the only chance of being ruined, beyond its present ruin.

Yet, though dead to all the purposes for which we live to-day, the place has its glorious recollections, and not merely rude and warlike ones, but those of brighter and milder triumphs, the fruits of which we still enjoy. Italy can count several of these lifeless towns, which, four or five hundred years ago, were each the birth-place of its own school of art; nor have they yet forgotten to be proud of the dark, old pictures, and the faded frescoes, the pristine beauty of which was a light and gladness to the world. But now, unless one happens to be a painter, these famous works make us miserably desperate. They are poor, dim ghosts of what, when Giotto or Cimabue first created them, threw a splendour along the stately aisles; so far gone towards nothingness, in our day, that scarcely a hint of design or expression can glimmer through the dusk. Those early artists did well to paint their frescoes. Glowing on the church walls, they might be looked upon as symbols of the living spirit that made Catholicism a true religion, and that glorified it as long as it retained a genuine life; they filled the transepts with a radiant throng of saints and angels, and threw around the high altar a faint reflection—as much as mortals could see, or bear—of a Diviner Presence. But, now that the colours are so wretchedly bedimmed—now that blotches of plastered wall dot the frescoes all over, like a mean reality thrusting itself through life's brightest illusions—the next best artist to Cimabue, or Giotto, or Ghirlandaio, or Pinturicchio, will be he that shall reverently cover their ruined masterpieces with whitewash!

Kenyon, however, being an earnest student and critic of Art, lingered long before these pathetic relics; and Donatello, in his present phase of penitence, thought no time spent amiss while he could be kneeling before an altar. Whenever they found a cathedral, therefore, or a Gothic church, the two travellers were of one mind to enter it. In some of these holy edifices they saw pictures that time had not dimmed nor injured in the least, though they perhaps belonged to as old a school of Art as any that were perishing around them. These were the painted windows; and, as often as he gazed at them, the sculptor blessed the mediæval time, and its gorgeous contrivances of splendour; for surely the skill of man has never accomplished, nor his mind imagined, any other beauty or glory worthy to be compared with these.

It is the special excellence of pictured glass, that the light, which falls merely on the outside of other pictures, is here interfused throughout the work; it illuminates the design, and invests it with a living radiance; and, in requital, the unfading colours transmute the common daylight into a miracle of richness and glory, in its passage through the heavenly substance of the blessed and angelic shapes which throng the high-arched window.

"It is a woeful thing," cried Kenyon, while one of these frail, yet enduring and fadeless pictures threw its hues on his face, and on the pavement of the church around him,—"a sad necessity that any Christian soul should pass from earth without once seeing an antique painted window, with the bright Italian sunshine glowing through it! There is no other such true symbol of the glories of the better world, where a celestial radiance will be inherent in all things and persons, and render each continually transparent to the sight of all."

"But what a horror it would be," said Donatello, sadly, "if there were a soul among them through which the light could not be transfused."

"Yes; and perhaps this is to be the punishment of sin," replied the sculptor; "not that it shall be made evident to the universe, which can profit nothing by such knowledge, but that it shall insulate the sinner from all sweet society by rendering him impermeable to light, and, therefore, unrecognizable in the abode of heavenly simplicity and truth. Then, what remains for him, but the dreariness of infinite and eternal solitude."

"That would be a horrible destiny, indeed!" said Donatello.

His voice, as he spoke the words, had a hollow and dreary cadence, as if he anticipated some such frozen solitude for himself. A figure in a dark robe was lurking in the obscurity of a side-chapel close by, and made an impulsive movement forward, but hesitated as Donatello spoke again.

"But there might be a more miserable torture than to be solitary for ever," said he. "Think of having a single companion in eternity, and instead of finding any consolation, or, at all events, variety of torture, to see your own weary, weary sin repeated in that inseparable soul!"

"I think, my dear count, you have never

read Dante," observed Kenyon. "That idea is somewhat in his style, but I cannot help regretting that it came into your mind just then."

The dark-robed figure had shrunk back, and was quite lost to sight among the shadows of the chapel.

"There was an English poet," resumed Kenyon, turning again towards the window, "who speaks of the 'dim, religious light,' transmitted through painted glass. I always admired this richly descriptive phrase; but, though he was once in Italy, I question whether Milton ever saw any but the dingy pictures in the dusty windows of English cathedrals, imperfectly shown by the gray English daylight. He would else have illuminated that word, 'dim,' with some epithet that should not chase away the dimness, yet should make it glow like a million of rubies, sapphires, emeralds, and topazes. Is it not so with yonder window? The pictures are most brilliant in themselves, yet dim with tenderness and reverence, because God himself is shining through them."

"The pictures fill me with emotion, but not such as you seem to experience," said Donatello. "I tremble at those awful saints, and, most of all, at the figure above them. He glows with Divine wrath!"

"My dear friend," exclaimed Kenyon, "how strangely your eyes have transmuted the expression of the figure! It is divine love, not wrath."

"To my eyes," said Donatello, stubbornly, "it is wrath, not love! Each must interpret for himself."

The friends left the church, and, looking up from the exterior, at the window which they had just been contemplating within, nothing was visible but the merest outline of dusky shapes. Neither the individual likeness of saint, angel, nor Saviour, and far less the combined scheme and purport of the picture, could anywise be made out. That miracle of radiant art, thus viewed, was nothing better than an incomprehensible obscurity, without a gleam of beauty to induce the beholder to attempt unravelling it. "All this," thought the sculptor, "is a most forcible emblem of the different aspect of religious truth and sacred story, as viewed from the warm interior of belief, or from its cold and dreary outside. Christian faith is a grand cathedral, with divinely pictured windows. Standing without, you see no glory, nor can possibly imagine any; standing within, every ray of light reveals a harmony of unspeakable splendours."

After Kenyon and Donatello emerged from the church, however, they had better opportunity for acts of charity and mercy than for religious contemplation; being immediately surrounded by a swarm of beggars, who are the present possessors of Italy, and share the spoil of the stranger with the fleas and mosquitoes, their formidable allies. These pests—the human ones—had hunted the two travellers at every stage of their journey. From village to village

ragged boys and girls kept almost under
the horses' feet; hoary grandsires and grand-
dams caught glimpses of their approach, and
hobbled to intercept them at some point of
vantage; blind men stared them out of countenance with their sightless orbs; women held
up their unwashed babies; cripples displayed
their wooden legs, their grievous scars, their
dangling, boneless arms, their broken backs,
their burden of a hump, or whatever infirmity
or deformity Providence had assigned them for
an inheritance. On the highest mountain summit
—in the most shadowy ravine—there was a
beggar waiting for them. In one small village,
Kenyon had the curiosity to count merely how
many children were crying, whining, and bellow-
ing all at once for alms. They proved to be
more than forty of as ragged and dirty little
imps as any in the world; besides whom all the
wrinkled matrons, and most of the village maids,
and not a few stalwart men, held out their hands,
grimly, piteously, or smilingly, in the forlorn

hope of whatever trifle of coin might remain in pockets already so fearfully taxed. Had they been permitted, they would gladly have knelt down and worshipped the travellers, and have cursed them, without rising from their knees, if the expected boon failed to be awarded.

Yet they were not so miserably poor but that the grown people kept houses over their heads. In the way of food, they had, at least, vegetables in their little gardens, pigs and chickens to kill, eggs to fry into omelets with oil, wine to drink, and many other things to make life comfortable. As for the children, when no more small coin appeared to be forthcoming, they began to laugh and play, and turn heels over head, showing themselves jolly and vivacious brats, and evidently as well fed as need be. The truth is, the Italian peasantry look upon strangers as the almoners of Providence, and therefore feel no more shame in asking and receiving alms, than in availing themselves of providential bounties in whatever other form.

In accordance with his nature, Donatello was always exceedingly charitable to these ragged battalions, and appeared to derive a certain consolation from the prayers which many of them put up in his behalf. In Italy a copper coin of minute value will often make all the difference between a vindictive curse, death by apoplexy being the favourite one, mumbled in an old witch's toothless jaws, and a prayer from the same lips, so earnest that it would seem to reward the charitable soul with at least a puff of grateful breath, to help him heavenward. Good wishes being so cheap, though possibly not very efficacious, and anathemas so exceedingly bitter, even if the greater portion of their poison remain in the mouth that utters them, it may be wise to expend some reasonable amount in the purchase of the former. Donatello invariably did so; and as he distributed his alms under the pictured window, of which we have been speaking, no less than seven ancient women lifted their hands and besought blessings on his head.

"Come," said the sculptor, rejoicing at the happier expression which he saw in his friend's face, "I think your steed will not stumble with you to-day. Each of these old dames looks as much like Horace's Atra Cura as can well be conceived; but, though there are seven of them, they will make your burden on horseback lighter instead of heavier."

"Are we to ride far?" asked the count.

"A tolerable journey betwixt now and tomorrow noon," Kenyon replied; "for, at that hour, I purpose to be standing by the Pope's statue in the great square of Perugia."

END OF VOL. II.